my mother, my madness

ISBN 978-1-928476-36-8
ebook 978-1-928476-37-5

Deep South, Makhanda
contact@deepsouth.co.za
www.deepsouth.co.za

Distributed in South Africa by
University of KwaZulu-Natal Press
www.ukznpress.co.za

Distributed worldwide by
African Books Collective
PO Box 721, Oxford, OX1 9EN, UK
www.africanbookscollective.com/publishers/deep-south

Cover art: Carla Kreuser
Text design and layout: Liz Gowans

my mother, my madness

Colleen Higgs

For Sean, Michael, and Geraldine

2009

The yellow-stained room
6 September

My mother Sally lives in an assisted-living care centre near Century City in Cape Town. She has a small one-bedroomed apartment with a kitchenette, a living area, and a bathroom with a shower and handrail in it. From her bedroom and the living room she has a full view of Table Mountain. She objects to the Centre calling itself a Luxury Retirement Resort as the billboards near the entrance proclaim.

I manage her life for her. I pay her bills, organise doctor's appointments, and sort out problems. Once a month I buy her what she needs online from Pick n Pay. She eats all her meals downstairs in the dining room, where waiters serve the residents their three course meals. The tables are laid with linen. My mother complains about the food, "They're always giving us fish," she says, "I don't like fish." Omelettes are offered as a substitute. "And I don't like omelettes."

Each month I buy her snacks, four packs of 9 double ply toilet rolls, the *You* magazine, Cokes – 70 x 2 litre bottles for the month, and cigarettes, seven cartons of Rothmans 30s – the blue pack. And shampoo, tissues, soap, toothpaste, shower gel, roll-on deodorant, facecloths, body lotion, moisturiser, depending on what she needs or has run out of.

My mother's fingernails are stained yellow from nicotine and the cream coloured paint around the doorframe entrance to her apartment is also stained yellow.

There is a gym in the resort's health centre, with a swimming pool, and gardens to walk in, but my mother spends most of her time sitting in her recliner smoking, drinking Coke and watching TV on her big flat screen. She doesn't use the gym or the gardens.

Terrible news
16 September

Forgot to take my meds on Monday, so by yesterday morning felt really peculiar: over-tired, wobbly, achy. If I ever come off them, I'll have to do so under supervision and make sure it's in a period where not too much is expected of me work-wise. Much better today.

Terrible news, the best friend of one of my friends shot herself on Tuesday night. Her son killed himself in February and she had been battling terribly with the unbearable loss, overwhelming grief and depression. Maybe that's also why I was feeling so weird yesterday. Even though I wasn't close to J, we had worked together and she was in my outer circle of friends and colleagues. When I heard the news that her son had killed himself I wondered how she would ever recover.

I think of my mother and her many suicide attempts, I'm thankful she was not ever successful.

Shitty dreams
29 September

Last night I dreamt about my mother. I was still living with her, with my three siblings (we are all in our forties now, I am the oldest). In the dream we were in our teens and twenties, and the older of my two brothers, Sean, lived upstairs. The toilet got blocked and started to overflow, and a brown liquid stain started to appear along the edges of the ceiling and down the kitchen wall. My mother got dressed for work, oblivious. I begged her to do something about it, but she calmly set off for work as usual. Later on a plumber arrived. We had to throw away all the food in the kitchen cupboards and clean them out and wash the soiled containers.

I must remember to phone and book an appointment with my mother's psychiatrist. Her previous one has gone to Canada for 18 months. So she now is seeing a psychiatrist nearer to where she lives. He wants to interview me for background on her. Even though he has her file and case notes, he wants more information, from the horse's mouth, he says. Not sure if I am the horse or my mother is.

I need to pay her levy for the Centre in the next few days. Most of her other bills, apart from the pharmacy bills, come off her account automatically — the DSTV, the phone bill, the bank charges and some others that I forget now. I pay her insurance once a year. The insurance is not expensive, as her life has been reduced to few possessions.

It's peculiar managing someone else's life. Having that kind of responsibility but at the same time how mundane much of it is.

Sometimes she phones me.

"When you going to visit me again?"

9

"I'm not sure."

"Well I need toilet paper."

"OK, well ask Chantel and I will send some with your order on Friday."

She uses at least one roll of double ply toilet paper a day. Is that a lot? It seems to be. And always she runs out. However much I buy for her, it is never quite enough.

The last time I shopped, Chantel asked me to buy Sunlight dishwashing liquid for her. Her carer washes her Coke glasses and her ashtray. When I visited two Sundays ago, Chantel told me that my mother had poured the whole bottle of Sunlight down the drain. When I asked Sally why she had done this, she said, "What do I need this crap for?"

My thoughts exactly, Mom.

Opting out
30 September

I'm seeing my mother's psychiatrist next Wednesday afternoon. It will take me half an hour to drive there, up Koeberg Road, into Milnerton, half an hour to see him and then half an hour to get home.

Why does she see a psychiatrist? Not easy to answer simply. She has been diagnosed as bipolar. She has also suffered from depression, which goes with the bipolar. She attempted suicide several times in her life, many times. She never took her meds in any kind of systematic fashion, and now, for the first time in her life, her meds are administered to her. Even so she has been known to hide them, throw them away, flush them down the toilet. Now the carers crush them into her yoghurt to ensure she takes them.

When she first saw the apartment she would be moving to, she burst into tears. After a few minutes she went to the windows and looked down and said, "Oh well, I guess I could jump out of the window if I really hate it here." She sobbed all the way home. I felt terrible; guilty and sad. But I was firm with her. "If you are going to say things like that, we will have to find a different kind of place for you to live." One with barred windows, I thought to myself.

Now she lives there in the Luxury Retirement Resort. "It's too far away," she says.

Too far from where? Fish Hoek, probably, where she used to live. But it is also as good as it gets, for someone who gave up a long time ago, perhaps for reasons beyond her control, and who now can't or won't manage her own life.

Before this she moved to live with my brother, Sean, after living alone in her Fish Hoek Genoa Road house for several years. David, her husband, died in early 2000. David, my dad, my stepfather, her husband. After that, it was downhill. It was clear he had been containing her for the last decade or so. He did all the shopping, cooking and chores. My mother gardened and did pottery; she had her own kiln. She carried on gardening in Genoa Road. But there were also disturbing phone calls where she sounded drunk, but actually because she had taken too many pills of one kind or another. Sleeping pills, painkillers.

A deeply unsatisfying love affair

My whole life has felt like a long deeply unsatisfying love affair with my mother. She is the beloved who doesn't love back. She is too caught up in her own dramas and unhappiness. She is the one who waits to be made happy and it is an impossible task. Reading *Jelly Dog Days*, the new novel by Erica Emdon, put me in mind of her. (Most things do, either as a stark contrast or as a resonating similarity.) The things that she and Lizette in the novel had in common were numerous. They both had children way too early, Lizette at seventeen and my mother at twenty. She 'fell pregnant' at nineteen. Falling pregnant sounds like you tripped or lost your balance. Both mothers are narcissistic and self-involved. Terry (the oldest girl in the novel) had to cook and look after her younger siblings while her mother got pissed most nights. My mother wasn't as extreme as Lizette, but I do remember from the age of 13 cooking quite often and looking after my siblings, and worrying about my mom. One school holiday when I was 14 my parents left me in charge of my siblings in our flat in Yeoville, I had to make sure they stayed inside and didn't get into trouble. I remember spending a day sitting at the front door. I'm not sure how it went after that. I've gone blank.

My mother didn't drink alcohol. She has always been a Coke and cigarettes person. She got into smoking dope at one stage for a couple of years; it was in Maseru, the early 70s and there was a band that played at the Holiday Inn, The Los Indonesios. I found out years later that my mother had an affair with the lead singer, Nico.

Does she wash her hair with conditioner?
2 October

The bill came for her levy. I usually wait a couple of days before paying. Partly I'm being passive aggressive, partly procrastinating. Maybe the two are the same thing? Leaping at doing something for my mother is not something that happens spontaneously. I have to drag myself by the hand cajoling, wheedling, and make myself do the things I need to do. Have to do. Must do. Have agreed to do. Have taken it upon myself to do.

She had two haircuts last month, two trips to the hairdresser. Since she has been living at the Luxury Retirement Resort her hair always looks straggly and greasy. At first I wondered if she was washing it with conditioner. I don't buy her conditioner anymore, so it can't be that. Her hair is now completely grey, and never looks groomed or well cut. Could be that the hairdresser at the Luxury Retirement Resort is hopeless.

My mother looks like a bergie when I pick her up to take her out. She wears baggy well-worn jeans with an elasticised waist, beach shoes with velcroed straps across her feet. Her toenails are always too long. She is reluctant to allow anyone to touch her feet. It makes her giggle and she is squeamish about it. Her T-shirt or blouse is usually crumpled, slightly stained. I take her shopping for new clothes every 6 months or so, for a few new items. She either doesn't wear them or she quickly manages to make them look crumpled and stained too. She cuts the sleeves off her pajamas with a pair of nail scissors.

An old friend of hers visited her recently, and afterwards she phoned me, "Coll, you must do something about your mother." She tried tactfully to tell me all the things I know already. What can I say?

Dear Elizabeth
3 October

My mother's medical aid claims emails arrive in my inbox. 'Dear Elizabeth' the claims say, using a name she has never been known by. She was always Sally. Her second name is Sally.

Maybe there is more than one of her, an Elizabeth and a Sally. I'm a receiving station, a clearing house for all of Sally's problems and troubles, claims and payments, woes and needs, complaints, sadnesses, despair, discomforts and small pleasures.

Most of the medical aid claims are for the pharmacy. She takes a lot of meds: for blood pressure, bipolar, sleeping pills, calcium, cholesterol, and other meds too, about 8 different ones three times a day.

Twice since she's been at the Luxury Retirement Resort, she has had a dizzy, vomiting spell where she's been nursed in the frail care centre, the ground floor of the LRR's Care Centre. The frail care centre frightens her, she can see it's death row and she hates it. Unless she's really sick she won't go there. Visiting her there foreshadows for me what will come next. She looks softer and more vulnerable when she's in one of their hospital beds, slightly elevated.

Currency
4 October

A headache woke me this morning, all night it nagged through my sleep, an unpleasant tugging. Most Sundays I wonder if I should fetch Sally and bring her home to me for lunch. Most Sundays I decide not to. Today perhaps not. Every Sunday I tussle with myself. Maybe next Sunday. A headache and my mother, no − too much for one day. Also extra children this morning and the dismal sadness of Sundays. I prefer the structure of weekdays, they are more containing. Sundays are too open-ended for me. Usually. I must pay my mother's levy today. And her pharmacy bill.

It is her money; I have power of attorney and signing powers on her bank account. If Sally had to manage her money, she would give it away, buy even more cigarettes. Though heavens knows what she would do with them. My prodigal mother. Perhaps she doesn't smoke 90 a day; perhaps she uses the cigarettes as a kind of currency. To get her carer to hang around more, or to curry favours with the waiters? Perhaps her toilet paper is also a currency.

She likes having me manage her affairs. She is finally able

to give up all semblance of taking responsibility for herself.
"I don't have any money," she says, "you will have to ask my
daughter."

Still procrastinating
5 October

Still haven't paid Sally's levy. Will do it tomorrow, I promise
myself. It's not that hard, I just have to be in the right
headspace. Also need to do online Pick n Pay shopping
for home. Maybe tomorrow. Some things you have to
procrastinate. No good doing them when you are too tired,
too overwhelmed.

Haven't thought much about Sally today, been too busy.
I prefer the busyness of Mondays, of weekdays, to the quiet
desperation of Sundays.

Later on: Paid the levy. I said to myself, as I sat down at
my desk this morning. You can do it. Also paid the R25.60,
which was owing to my mother's previous psychiatrist
for about three months. Now I can face the week, having
cleared out some nagging guilt by ticking off my to-do list.

Seeing someone
I go and see my own psychologist today at noon,
Renee. She is a Jungian, very skilled and calm. I've
been seeing her for about four years. I've learnt so
much from her, especially about being objective about
despair, my own complexes, and myself. Especially
my mother complex. How to manage the anxiety that

often threatens to overwhelm me.

I've been in therapy/analysis for most of my adult life. I started in 1986, in Joburg, the woman I saw was in her early thirties I think, a Freudian, Kleinian therapist. I saw her for seven years. Then I moved to Grahamstown and saw Margaret Anema, a legendary figure of strange practices. I could write a book about her. Her social circle and intimates were all people who were either in therapy with her or had been. For a couple of years when I was very broke, I used to cook for her as a way to pay her. This was her suggestion. A sangoma model of healing. I also did chores, not in direct payment, but as a way of paying her back for being there for me. For loving me. She gave me gifts, a beautiful mohair rug, a writing desk and chair that had been in her family for generations.

When I moved to Cape Town, I had phone therapy with Margaret for a few years. I used to talk to her on the phone at 5.30 in the morning, once a week. While in the grip of a particularly dark bout of depression, I knew that I needed to "see someone".

I take anti-depressants; have done for two and a half years. They have helped stabilise my mood, and I don't slosh about in grumpy irritation and snappishness. I have calm, even-keeled days where I get things done. Thanks to my analyst and our work, I am now self-employed, which I love. I started a small publishing company. Money is tighter, but everything else is looser, easier, and the desire to work flows easily from inside me.

Margaret's advice had been to protect myself and cut ties with my mother. Renee encouraged me to take on the responsibility of looking after her. There have been things to sort out, like who should do what for her. Lentils and stones. I'm still doing the sorting out internally, but most of the practical stuff is in place.

The freedom of a schedule
7 October

Going to see Sally's psychiatrist today. My husband Adam asks why he needed to see me. "Apparently he needs background." Sally is something of an unreliable narrator. Perhaps I am too. There is a form to fill in for Sally. I will be glad to have this chore over with. But, I think, it will never be over. There will always be another chore. So I am trying to think instead. This is what I am doing just for today. Anxiety nibbles away at me, a mouse eating at my insides.

Perhaps I don't have to have the Sunday blues every week wondering if I should see my mother, visit her, have her over to lunch. But if I schedule a fixed visit once a month, I would be freed of worrying and angsting every Sunday. But then, which Sunday? What about the third Sunday of the month, I'm thinking. I will let Sally know, and my brothers, and hope they might do something similar. Sometimes I think she doesn't deserve any of this, yet I still feel compassionate towards her. It's such an odd concoction of love, guilt, duty, anger, resentment, longing.

A history of madness
8 October

The trip to my mother's psychiatrist was odder than I could have imagined. I arrived to find Sally sitting in the waiting room. I wasn't expecting her. I think the receptionist must have thought I was making the appointment for my mother. So Sally did see the doctor and I waited and read crappy magazines. No recent magazines at all, and mostly corporate hospital publications. The radio played softly all the time. I told the doctor finally, after waiting an hour, that I was annoyed at having my time wasted. He was apologetic and we moved on. He likes my mother, has seen her three times. He thinks she is a bit bored and thought perhaps we could get a companion for her, who would take her out and do things with her three times a week or so. My heart sinks. The work involved.

He asked me to write down a brief history of her mental illness. Here it is:

Sally's first big trauma was at the age of 7. Her parents, who lived in Selukwe, in what was then Southern Rhodesia, "gave her away" to her childless aunt and uncle, Ailsa and Iain, who lived in what was then Basutoland. She didn't see her parents again till she was 38. The reunion was organised by her sisters who had not been given away. After that meeting she plummeted into a deep depression.

When she was in high school, she got into trouble for stealing; she was at Eunice Girls High in Bloemfontein, as a boarder. She left school at the end of Std 9 and went nursing in Cape Town. During her second year of nursing, she had a bad car accident, and soon afterwards she got pregnant, at age 19. She then moved to Joburg and joined up with her second boyfriend, Philip, and married him. She wasn't sure whether boyfriend number one or two was my father, or if she did she never told me with clarity, but I did find out that boyfriend 1 was 18 and a first year student at UCT while boyfriend 2 was doing his accounting articles in Johannesburg, although she knew him in Cape Town.

When I was twenty-one months old she had another baby, Sean. Then she had a nervous breakdown (as they used to call it) at age 23, for which she was hospitalised for 6 weeks. After this interlude she went to Mozambique with her friend, Vivian, whose parents had a holiday house near Lourenço Marques, now Maputo, for another 6 weeks to recover. Sean and I were sent to her in-laws in Kimberley for that period. Her husband, Philip was still in Johannesburg, but as we know single dads don't manage children and jobs at the same time. Especially not in the early 1960s. Shortly after all of this, my mother decided to divorce Philip. A custody battle ensued. While this was going on, she met David, and married him just a few months after first meeting him. He insisted on taking her "to fetch your kids" from the in-laws and drove her to Kimberley to retrieve us.

When I was 5½, she had my second brother, Michael, and then another baby when I was 7½, my sister Geraldine, whom we have always called Gerry.

The first time that my mother tried to commit suicide (that I was aware of) was while she was pregnant with Gerry.

Over the years there were numerous other instabilities and ordeals.

Sean had a hard time in his late teens and twenties. He went into the military at age 17 and then started smoking dagga, and taking other drugs. The next ten years were distressing for the whole family as he too was unstable and had many traumatic experiences, which often involved my parents or other family members rescuing him, or trying to. He was hospitalised at Valkenberg for six weeks in his early 20s. After that he spent some time living on the streets and busking.

My mother had a violent temper that over the years involved throwing things, shouting, breaking things, threatening to leave, and actually leaving at least once.

She suffered from migraines and back pain and neck pain from a whiplash injury in her late 20s. She became addicted to painkillers, and when she was in her late 50s, after my stepfather David's death, she took this to new levels. She obtained sleeping pills by misusing prescriptions. She frequently took far too many sleeping pills and painkillers, and would sleep for a couple of days.

She was admitted to hospital a number of times for psychiatric reasons over the years, in periods from a few days to several weeks in various hospitals at different times. She has been diagnosed as bipolar by two psychiatrists in Cape Town. I am not sure what her diagnostic history was before, as I was not managing her care then.

She declined rapidly after David died, stopped eating properly, frequently overdosed on over-the-counter medications, and she didn't take care of herself. She was known to go to the shops in Fish Hoek in her pajamas. At one point she was admitted to the Kenilworth Clinic for three weeks.

After that she went to live in the house next door to Sean. She had two carers while living there, neither of whom was good for her. The first was a bully and the second was manipulative and made constant attempts to get money out of my mother, and me.

After much anguish and discussion with my sister in particular, we decided to buy her an apartment in the High Care Centre of the Luxury Retirement Resort. Just before she went to live there, she was admitted to the Kenilworth Clinic for two weeks to give her some structured input and support before she moved to the LRR.

Insisting on driving
9 October

I dreamt about Sally last night. And about my grandmother, who I later understood was actually my great aunt (from the age of 7 my mother was raised by her aunt and uncle, so we knew them as granny and grandpa).

In the dream, Sally arrived at my flat. She was younger than she is now and could drive, whereas my gran was very old and frail and needed managing. We argued about where to go and what to do. I insisted on driving. That's where the dream ends.

When she was younger, she was a fast, good driver; she

hated being driven, especially by David. He was a good driver too, but a little too dreamy for her. She often shouted at him and was a vociferous back seat driver if he was at the wheel.

She no longer drives. Old people recede and become less capable and coordinated, the tide going out.

She breaks my heart. I'm still thinking about seeing her on Wednesday. Clearly she wants something more from me, but not enough to know what it is, to be able to visualise it, to articulate it. She only knows how to complain, to say what she doesn't want, what she doesn't like. She doesn't know how to say what she does like or want. Apart from the obvious things like Coke and cigarettes.

Giving permission
10 October

Yesterday, Chantel called me, "Is it OK for Mrs. Higgs to have a guest for lunch?" (They will add it to her tab.) Of course it is OK. So strange to field such requests, as though I was the parent. The guest was a friend of my parents from Lesotho days. She lives in Cape Town now, and sometimes takes my mother out to lunch.

Chantel also wanted to know if I'd paid the levy. Yes, I did, I said. But because of fears about my own memory loss I checked and emailed her the details.

To Let signs
12 October

This Sunday I didn't feel guilty about my mother, or not debilitatingly so. A light breeze, instead of a storm. Haven't finished the mental health history, but will send it as it is and the psychiatrist can ask questions.

While driving down Koeberg Road to his rooms in Milnerton, I noticed how so many used car dealers have closed down. There are all these empty lots with To Let on them, the cheerful flags gone, the cars gone, just concreted space. If you are a pigeon racer there is a shop on that road where you can buy supplies. I didn't stop the car and investigate, but I'm guessing – seed? cages? tags for their ankles? Maybe there are special oils to improve the condition of their feathers. The other thing I noticed was an Adult video store. Private cubicles and comfortable chairs?

"A steady bargain with the way things are" (Adrienne Rich)
14 October

I'm feeling less sorry for myself, less burdened, there are more choices as to how to deal with Sally and my responsibilities. The worst feeling is that trapped feeling, where you have responsibilities and cannot escape. My mother, my albatross. Beginning to feel less trapped. And to feel more compassion for myself, and for her too.

Getting rid of all the old crap
15 October

Last night I dreamt that my mother was moving and getting rid of most of her stuff. It was an upstairs apartment, quite large, with very steep narrow stairs to the front door. Lots of her stuff was trash, too damaged to even take to a second hand furniture store in Koeberg Road.

She had given some of her nicest things to Camilla, the wife of my first serious boyfriend. Camilla got a dressing table, its mirror showing age marks. She also got other furniture, including a sideboard. I was puzzled in the dream as to what claim Camilla had to my mother's things. Yet I was overwhelmed at seeing my mother's life reduced to so much flotsam and jetsam, it was hard for me to lay claim to anything of value.

My role was to organise the removal of the junk, the dirt, the cardboard boxes, the broken things, the mouldy mattress, the crap. I had men to help. The task kept growing and seemed to have no end. There was more and more old crap to get rid of.

Do you remember chocolate cigarettes?
17 October

Buzzy and busy day yesterday. Some good things have been coming into my life, along with the painful things, like the news of J's suicide.

An email from Chantel, "Please order cigarettes and

25

Cokes for Mom, she only has enough till next weekend." I usually order after the 25th when her pension money comes into her account. Will drop them off, I personally have to deliver her cigarettes anyway, thanks to legislation designed to prevent under-agers from buying cigarettes online. Sigh. Good legislation I guess, but not good for me, right now.

Must put my mind to finding a companion for my mother, perhaps she will smoke less if she gets out more. I tried out the idea of the electronic cigarette with her, she wasn't interested – she wants her cigarettes, as they are, not some new-fangled thing. She was suspicious that I was trying to palm off something fake onto her. Like chocolate cigarettes, do you remember those? I'm sure they are illegal now in South Africa, and would be seen to be enticing children into smoking. They tasted awful anyway.

I've never smoked. I tried two cigarettes about 10 years apart, maybe 12 or 14 years apart. The first one was at Zoo Lake with friends. We were rowing on the boats and my friends were smokers (at age 14). They had a box of Cameos. I smoked a cigarette and felt fabulous, sophisticated and aroused, glamorous and devilishly rule-breaking, daring: all the things cigarette manufacturers and their advertisers want you to feel.

I didn't try another cigarette until I was in my 20s. This time it was a Camel on a beach in the Transkei, with my boyfriend, we were camping. The Camel was stale. Again I felt sexy and sophisticated, although I didn't like the taste in my mouth. Maybe I don't like feeling sophisticated and sexy? Or maybe I was scared I liked it too much. Or maybe I knew in my heart of hearts it was really an illusion. Whatever it was that prevented me from smoking more than those two cigarettes, I'm glad I never got hooked. There are so many potential holes of addiction to fall into and I'm glad that for me smoking was not one of them.

Christmas already
18 October

Having a quiet, pleasant day, not thinking too much about my mother. I did briefly entertain the idea of fetching her here for lunch or tea. But quickly decided against it.

I need a quiet day, been very busy, and now time for rest. The year is spinning towards its close quickly now. Will have to see if my brothers will have Sally for Christmas, as we are going away. Usually Mike has her. Makes me feel a little guilty that he does and that I'm out of town over the Christmas period.

Sacrifices have to be made
19 October

I'm supposed to rush off to Century City area today to drop off my mother's fix, otherwise she's going to run out of Coke and cigarettes before the end of the month. Just thought of a brilliant idea – I'm going to use the local courier service that I use for work purposes to drop the stuff off.

I feel like a clever dope dealer who's just found a new mule to do the drop-offs. Can hardly wait to rush off to Pick n Pay and buy the Cokes and smokes, just to show how it is done. Still have to book dentist appointments for Kate and me, and an eye appointment to get reading glasses.

I've invited Mike and his family for Sunday lunch with my mother. I have yet to break it to Adam; he doesn't love Sunday lunch with his mother-in-law. Still, sacrifices have to be made.

Are you cured yet?
20 October

Just got back from seeing Renee, my analyst. Still haven't been to Pick n Pay. I often feel quite tired after a session. I may have a rest in a few minutes. Why is it such hard work? Adam often says to me after a session, "Are you cured yet?"

When I see him today he says, "Did you hit the wall?" We speak different languages, different dialects. What does he mean?

More cigarettes and Coke
21 October

After my morning walk I went to do some errands and bought a carton of cigarettes, going to get my courier to drop them off for her and will buy another six cartons for Sunday after her money comes in. Have also done the Pick n Pay order online, so she can have Cokes, fifty 2-litre bottles. When I was looking up shampoo, the search first landed on pet shampoos. I thought, my mother as a pet, as dependent as a dog, without offering as much pleasure. Do I sound like a bitch?

I bought her a *You* magazine, chips and nuts and chocolate biscuits. I feel like a bad Mom myself buying her crap like that. It's not good for her, but it's what she wants. And the four packs of 9 rolls of double ply toilet paper. I can't understand how she uses so much toilet paper. Every time I order toilet paper for her I wonder about it.

I must email Chantel to let her know that the Cokes will be there tomorrow. I was at the Checkers centre in Rondebosch this morning and 'forgot' to buy Cokes, but then decided that it was too much to send Cokes with my courier. But as I walked past the bottle store downstairs next to the Post Office I considered it again. But I also didn't feel like going into the bottle store at 8.30 in the morning.

So much admin and chores and tasks to run my life, never mind my mother's. Still haven't heard from her psychiatrist.

The Scream
22 October

Last night I had a dream that woke me up, wide-awake and paralysed at the same time. In the dream a child had been violated by her mother or her grandmother in her mouth, and the dream was a reenactment to try and understand what had happened.

I wasn't sure if I was the child, the mother or the grandmother, or a neutral watcher, or all of them. It was dark and strange and the violation involved a sheet. When I was writing the dream down, I thought of Munch's painting.

The last scene of the dream involved a swimming pool, still in the dark and a metal frame over the pool, I was trying to get out from under the frame and out of the pool. My hat was trapped, and I was trying to get out with the hat and all, a struggle.

Drink a glass of water
23 October

Friday. A mild headache. "Drink water," I hear a voice in my head say. My mother was always good at giving both a diagnosis and a prescription. I can imagine an alternate life for her where she would have made a good doctor. Kate tells me I have similar skills. "You are like a chemist, Mommy. You have all these creams, and plasters, and pills and medicines." If she grazes her knee, I tend to her with an ointment. If her tummy hurts, I first recommend going to the toilet and then a glass of water and then a little lie down with me for five minutes of cuddling or just lying next to each other in a companionable way. If her throat is sore, drink water; take tissue salts – Ferrum Phos. I don't know if they really work, but I think paying attention to aches and pains and trying to understand the message does.

My mother has been both a source of consolation and a source of illness in my life. There was a period when I would get ill immediately after I saw her. I would come down with a sick migraine or become utterly exhausted and need a long nap. It's better now, usually a little rest, half an hour's lie down, is enough.

Adam thinks I spend my life lying down. It is not true. But there is a little truth in it. Lying on my bed is restorative, a chance to reconnect with the great good Mother. Who holds me, embraces me and contains me. Then I am able to go back out into the world and be brave and competent again.

This afternoon I am going to the doctor for a check-up and to have my blood pressure and cholesterol tested for my exercise programme. I am taking Kate too; she has two tiny warts on her neck. Most mysterious. She's also been complaining of a sore neck. Is it because her school bag is so heavy? Maybe our doctor will be able to diagnose at least part of the problem.

Contagious snails
24 October

Kate has two little viral 'warts' on her neck, they're called molluscana contagioso, apparently quite common in children. They go away by themselves. Contagious snails. She is a beautiful child, and these two little warts are her first blemishes. Life setting in.

I have many blemishes. One of the things I didn't realise about ageing was how you can get bumps and lumps under the skin, not just ordinary cellulite. Subcutaneous something or other. As though small rocks or boulders have stopped in the continuous movement of blood through one's body. A small damming up, the beginning of dying. Thickening.

Sluggishness. If I run my hand over the front of my thigh or down my back – there they are. I have about eight altogether. I had one under my armpit that became uncomfortable, and it kept making me think of breast cancer. I had it taken out, under local anaesthetic by a plastic surgeon, who also removed a mole on my jawline. My mother and grandmother called that mole a beauty spot, it was always bigger than a freckle and slightly raised. But after 40 it started getting bigger and sprouting hairs.

Mole: I think of moles that are very active in our garden at present. Spring is here and they burrow and burrow. Our lawn is not really a lawn in any usual understanding of the word. We live on the Cape Flats, the soil is sandy and every spring the 'lawn' bursts into an abundance of greenery (weeds). Summer is a low-grade warfare against too much sun, no rain, choking weeds, moles, and our dog, who digs holes in search of the moles.

It takes time to learn the difference between weeds and plants that you want to nurture. Sometimes it seems cruel and heartless to rip 'weeds' out of the soil, shake soil off the roots, throw them into a pile to die.

My mother was always a good gardener; she knew the names and habits of plants. She had green fingers. I say had, because she no longer gardens, and doesn't take much interest in gardens either. She can't remember the names of plants readily. She no longer likes to bend over to pull out a weed. Probably she can't bend over. Her hands are yellowed, nicotine-stained.

Mommy made a restaurant
25 October

A family Sunday, my brother came to lunch with his two children, he fetched my mother and took her back and bought her three cartons of Rothmans cigarettes from Checkers at Century City. There were only three cartons in the store. Where can one buy cigarettes wholesale? Makro?

A happy day, and I don't feel too tired after a day of my mother. I made a lovely lunch of slow-baked garlic chicken casserole, polenta, salad, and rolls. For pudding – vanilla ice cream and toppings – almond praline, malted chocolate balls a la Woollies, strawberries, and crushed ginger biscuits. Kate greeted everyone with, "Mommy has made a restaurant." She decorated the plates with rose petals.

After lunch, my brother and I chatted, my mother sat in an armchair and drank Coke, every now and then she went outside for a smoke. The children played chess. They only left at about 4.30. It was very pleasant, and a relief for it not to be all up to me. My brother's wife Gaye had gone to a work girls' get-together and Adam was working, he sometimes does on a Sunday. It was oddly intimate the lunch, and felt like home and family. Even though as I told Kate I haven't lived with my brother for almost 30 years, there was an old familiarity. We gossiped in a gentle way about people we know/knew and have reconnected with on Facebook.

My mother asked my brother four times about his house and where his in-laws are living. It was the only sign of her dementia. Otherwise she was a pleasure.

I noticed how I wasn't fixated on her and forgot that she was there some of the time, but when I did focus on her, I knew what she needed, the outside shade pulled down (the west sun was getting too hot for her), her Coke topped up, and so on. And then my attention would veer back to the present.

One of the people we spoke about apparently suffers from bipolar. My mother said loudly, "I'm supposed to have that too."

"Well, yes, and the reason you feel so okay these days is that you take your meds," I said.

"Do you think so?" she said, not sounding convinced.

On becoming a dragon
27 October

Still a little tired from family Sunday lunch. But OK. Just got back from analysis. Such a rewarding hour. Always takes me a moment to calm down and be there. My analyst's room is dark and cool. The clock, the armchair, the box of tissues. Her lovely warm presence. My dreams. My anxieties. My complexes. My mother. My madness.

A life long habit of fixating on my mother, worrying about her.

Feel determined to find more 'dragon' or 'lioness' energy. To growl. To bare my teeth.

Busy day already, am going to read and nap this afternoon. Have a small window of time to myself.

The elephant in the room
29 October

Forgot to take my meds the other day, Tuesday, so took them on Tuesday evening and at the usual time yesterday, felt odd all day, blue and out of sorts, on a short tether. Slept all afternoon. Thank God I can, but not great to feel so crap that you have to lie down. Back on track today, feel myself. Always too much to do, most of it cool, but then I start playing Word Twist, my little Facebook vice.

Read Maya Fowler's novel, *The Elephant in the Room*, this week. It reminded me of how I was as a teenager, trying to get on top of my life and obsessing about my weight and food. Seeing some foods as bad and some as good. Also a really boring place to be in, where pretty much all you think about is food, the food you really want and the food you are allowed to have, that is legit, and how thin or fat your thighs are. I remember wanting to cut off part of my thighs and my belly. I would run my hands over my body, imagining a blade that could slice the offending flesh away.

The mom in 'Elephant' was disconnected and switched off from her kids. To have two kids be anorexic and bulimic and for the youngest to die of bulimia.

I never was anorexic, or bulimic. But I did have an obsessive-compulsive eating disorder. It was a thick porridge of comfort eating, worrying about food, thinking about food, thinking about my weight and my body fantasies. I kept a food diary and wrote down the diet I was on, the rules of the diet, and then my failings. I endured a high protein diet; lots of boiled eggs and biltong, and one where I ate only apples and many other diets too. Fowler's novel captures that awful feeling of tiredness and weakness from not eating properly that I remember. As if life wasn't tough enough without us having to be so brutal to ourselves.

Sharon Stone in Bloemfontein
30 October

Month end and Sally's bills start rolling in, the pharmacy bills, the telephone bill, and the statement from the LRR. And so on. I've done her Pick n Pay shop for the month, but will have to get her more cigarettes before the end of November.

Sally had lunch guests twice last month. Audrey and Lily, both old friends of hers from Lesotho. My siblings and and I used to love Lily's husband, John; he was funny and kind, though on reflection now, as an adult, I wouldn't have liked him for a husband. I think Lily and John got divorced. I gathered that he drank a lot, and sometimes didn't come home at night, but slept over at the party. I think I heard gossip that he had affairs. According to my mother, Lily fancied David, my stepfather. I guess that is all water under the bridge now. Lily was attractive, tall, rangy, long sun streaked hair. She came with my mother to Bloemfontein once, I was at boarding school there. We had lunch at the President Hotel. First we sat in the lounge and had drinks. Lily sat opposite me, she was wearing a short dress and there was a Sharon Stone moment. At 11, I was both shocked and titillated to see that she wasn't wearing panties.

My mother used to smoke dagga with some of her friends; this was also a source of anxiety for me. At primary school, my best friend, Shirley, broke up with me about this issue, because it was all I would talk about. She got bored with me I guess. Being best friends in primary school was a bit like marriage. I was devastated by our 'divorce'.

Staying alive
2 November

So many chores; just being alive is a long work-in-progress, just being alive, staying alive (cue the Bee Gees).

So glad tomorrow is Tuesday and the day I see my analyst. It's always cheering to see her, reassuring. Sifting through the lentils and the stones with her, sorting things out, brightens my heart. At times I find it hard to figure out which is which. To trust myself. To be on my own side. My side is the one of the bad, hard-hearted girl. The cold one, the one who is not a good daughter, not a good friend, not a good wife, who guards her time and her energy preciously, ferociously.

Feel slightly beset tonight. Overwhelmed, overloaded. All day my inner weather has been changing for the worse. Colder, rainier, stormier, inclement.

I love Kate with all my heart, but I also wonder if I am a good mother, a good enough mother. Am I too soft? Am I failing her in her growth to independence? Am I keeping her crippled and needy of me? I don't want to do those things, but it's not always clear what one is doing, what is the right choice. At seven she still likes to, wants to, demands to be put to bed by one of us, tonight she tried having our dog, Perry, a golden retriever, on her bed. She didn't go to sleep till I finished Sally's online shopping.

It was meant to be her Dad putting her to bed tonight, but she wanted to try by herself. Her dad is a bit all or nothing and not prepared to engage in going-to-sleep experiments at 7 o'clock at night. I am endlessly flexible, and open to suggestion, and to finding a better way.

I feel like crying tonight. Sometimes my life feels full of loss and grief and tears.

While I was putting Kate to bed, I thought about the women's clothing shop, Robelle, in Pinelands that sells clothes for older women and larger sizes. I will have a look at it and perhaps buy some clothes for my mother there. She takes a size 44 or 46 in pants and 42 in tops. She has become heavier, more overweight than she has ever been, from no exercise and all that Coke, and the good food at the Luxury Retirement Resort.

Squadrons of helpers
4 November

Got an email from Chantel that my mother is about to run out of cigarettes. Have to figure out a way to get two cartons there by Sunday. I guess I could use the courier again. I am going to have tea with my mother on Wednesday next week, with a friend who also has a mother living in the complex, in one of the apartment blocks.

My friend just called and offered to deliver the cigarettes. At times I paint myself into a corner and find myself having to perform extraordinary conjuring tricks to get the things done that I have agreed to do. Other times I find I have squadrons of helpers of the best kind. One of my helpers at my business brought me flowers yesterday. She is a young woman who has been interning with me. She has been absolutely invaluable and yet she is thanking me.

Oh and I've booked tickets for Kate and me to see *The Nutcracker* at the Baxter on Saturday afternoon. We have read several different versions of the story and she is doing ballet for her second year. I am delighted, I almost feel as though my mother (my good fantasy mother) was taking me to the ballet. I'm thrilled to be going to the ballet with my girl. We have also read most of Noel Streatfield's books, many of which feature ballet.

A life of her own
6 November

Kate has gone to movie night at school for the Grade 1s to 4s; she went in her PJs and dressing gown and took her sleeping bag and four soft toys and R20, R10 for the movie and R10 for tuck-shop. She's starting to have her own life, separate from me. Her dad took her and our lift club family will bring her home. All these moments and days of life where things change.

I have paid my mother's levies on time this month, my

passive aggression let up. My friend will take her cigarettes to her on Sunday, mustn't forget to drop them off tomorrow.

Another good mother

On Sunday I am doing a 5km Fun Walk, been going to Walk for Life since the end of September and I've been loving it. The natural high from exercise is brilliant. The woman who runs the Rondebosch Run/Walk for Life, Naomi, is warm and encouraging, another good mother. Praises me, notices me, sees me, encourages. She herself is a good example, she is warm, and her body is gorgeous from exercise, she exudes good energy and kindness. It's a big deal for me to be doing a 5km walk.

There are so many alternative good parents out there to allow into one's heart. Bit by bit it repairs the damage. The best repair has been to figure out and learn to be a good mother to myself and to Kate, and to forgive myself when I make mistakes.

The Bad Tooth Fairy

11 November

I committed a huge sin of omission last night. Kate lost a tooth, and the tooth fairy forgot to come. When she came to tell me, with the evidence in her hand, I had to think quickly, at 6 this morning. I said, "You know what? I think the poor tooth fairy just couldn't make it in the storm we had last night, I'm sure she will come tonight." Kate sat down and wrote a letter to the tooth fairy, saying it was OK, but she hoped that she could come tonight.

I mustn't forget to remind that tooth fairy, there isn't much wiggle room left.

The long shadow

The after-effects of inadequate mothering have a long shadow; it becomes a lifelong condition one has to learn to live with. My sister and I have just had a difficult interaction that I think has its roots in the past and our respective mothering by Sally. We love each other and have a good relationship and have both worked hard in therapy for years. We were able to solve the issue, but it was a compromise for both of us, maybe even more for her.

My sister is eight years younger than me. When you are children, this is a big gap. I remember being deeply jealous of her. Our mother saw this, and inflamed it. I don't know if she did it consciously or not. I always had to let my sister sit in the front seat; understand her behaviour because she was the youngest. I was also expected to care for her at times, and to share my bedroom with her. Reflecting back, she had better mothering than I did, as she had a nanny who adored her and protected her and was there for her in a way that none of my mother's other children experienced. So the absent, depressed, narcissistic mothering she got from Sally was mitigated by her nanny. But she lost this good mother when we left Lesotho; she was in Grade 1, nearly 6 years old. That loss must have been painful, and possibly repressed quite quickly too. I think my mother has been surprised how my sister and I have become closer as adults.

I sent myself to boarding school at the age of 11. Deeply under the influence of Enid Blyton, I begged to go, and my parents agreed. I went to a convent in Bloemfontein for two years. I must have needed to dramatise the absence I already felt. Boarding school was hard, I was homesick, and it was a bit like a prison. Rules and regulations, hideous food and not quite enough of it – or at least a feeling of scarcity, nuns, set bed times, punishments.

My mother visited me in Bloemfontein at least once or twice a term, and these visits were the highlights of my life in that period. I had her to myself, we would go out for lunch and shopping. She was glamorous in those days, beautiful and sexy, only 31, 32. I loved being alone with her, having her full attention.

How guilty are you exactly?
14 November

Always too much to do, sometimes I feel like I'm gasping for air, hardly ever feel that I have it all done, all sorted. Today we had to change library books; my girl is devouring books. Washed her hair, got the gardener sorted out, bought new ballet shoes. The woman at the Fairy Shop asked me if I knew how to sew the elastics in, "Yes" I said, "I do." I thought to myself, I am an expert. This is her third pair this year; Kate's feet have grown three sizes in six months. From size 11 to 13½. Also took her to an extra ballet practice for the exam at the end of the month. It is her first badge.

I don't know anything about the rigours or disciplines of ballet. She wasn't crazy about the practice – afterwards she said, "I am the worst in the class, I don't want to do the ballet exam." Part of me wants to let her stop and not do the exam, but I also know it is better to persevere. Fetched a shirt I had made from Mnandi's, filled up with petrol, drew money to pay the gardener. Brought Kate home, made tea for us, weeded a bit, had a nap because I had a headache and a big function to go to tonight.

I haven't bought my mom the extra Cokes she needs, she's run out already. Should have done it today for it to get to her on Monday. There are Coke tins at the LRR, so she won't do without.

Today was like one of those dreams where you are running but you don't get anywhere, you make no progress. I managed to buy a gift for tomorrow's party, and two Xmas presents. We're going away and there will be other children there too.

I feel guilty that I haven't phoned my mom and that I won't and nor will I see her soon. But not so guilty that I actually pick up the phone.

Biting and chewing

16 November

I had to ask someone to help me with my child today. I had an important meeting that had taken huge amounts of arranging to set up, and needed to be agreed with three people. Adam was unavailable – working, my Grade 1 daughter had nearly two hours between school and ballet. So I asked Katrien who lives right near the school if Kate could go home with her and her daughter today. She was so kind and easy about it. All worked well, she gave Kate lunch and she did homework with her. I feel weak with gratitude.

It felt like I had been mothered today. I always 'bite off more than I can chew' or juggle madly all the things I'm doing. Adam said today, "There is one phrase I can't stand to hear you say, I'm doing my best." Why is that? Is it a weak statement from someone who is not quite getting her act together? Someone making excuses for not being good enough?

Sometimes I wonder what it must be like to have a mother who could help me, who could babysit, a mother who could fetch Kate. It might feel a bit like today felt, only perhaps I wouldn't appreciate it as much, because I would probably take it for granted in the way that the well-mothered do.

Last minute rush

17 November

Going to be away from home for a few days, and am in a

mild state of panic. Have only just booked the airport shuttle for tomorrow, had to deal with a few different companies before I found one that was available. Can't find my suitcase in the garage and feel as though I could do with a stiff drink.

Had to buy a gift for Saturday's birthday girl, organised lifts for Kate – there and back (her dad is working on Saturday, again). Two toyshops later and I got a baby's bottle for a prop for her ballet exam, and a small basket for the same exam.

I had to persuade Kate to go to school today. She didn't want to swim, because her arms are sore and the water is too cold.

I'm sure there are hundreds of things I've forgotten to do, but so be it.

Waves of nostalgia
24 November

Been home for a few days, and have a list of things to do for my mother. I need to make a final insurance payment for this year, but first need to check that I have the correct amount. She ran out of cigarettes yesterday, but Chantel was willing to accept a payment and to organise a carton. I'm going to visit her on Wednesday afternoon with my friend whose mother lives in the area. So will try and buy cigarettes then.

This past weekend I was in Joburg and spent a bit of time in Parkhurst where we lived when I was in high school in the late 70s. It's almost unrecognisable, lots of double storey houses, very gentrified. We lived in 17th Street, 8th Street and

13th Street. Parkhurst these days is a lush neighbourhood, gorgeous gardens, huge trees, birds, glistening and vibrating with life. I was struck by how wide the streets in Joburg are. Lots of Cape Town streets are quite narrow in comparison. When we lived in Parkhurst it was a lower middle class neighbourhood. The houses were all on an eighth of an acre and had been built for returning servicemen at the end of World War 2. There are still some unrenovated original houses, but not many, and some shops that were there in the 70s – the bottle store, the stationery shop, a haberdashery shop. Being there was a heady mixture of strangeness, newness, seeing the familiar anew, and nostalgia.

This morning taking Kate and her classmate to school (we have a one week on, one week off lift club) they were talking about stickers and swapping stickers. Her friend asked Kate about where various stickers came from. It so interests me, their collecting. The stickers aren't useful in any way. The aim is to collect as many as possible, and as wide a range as possible. There are 3-Ds, jellies, glittery ones, dress up doll stickers, glow in the dark, cute puppy stickers and so on. The more unusual stickers you have, the more power you have to swop. I guess one day you just get tired of the whole thing and the sticker book disappears or gets relegated into a box or a shelf, and isn't looked at again for years, decades perhaps. Until one day you are older, and you find it, and a wave of nostalgia sweeps over you as you page through the plastic folder looking at your long forgotten old friends. Or your mom throws it away when you aren't looking.

Standing and falling
25 November

Does this happen to anyone else, I wonder? The feeling of being filled with purpose, lots to do, and then an attack of feeling overwhelmed, immobilised? I try to keep the feelings of collapse at bay. To move swiftly onto a better thought, but sometimes I fail.

Yesterday, after analysis, I managed to keep going till 3, then I had to lie down, utterly exhausted. I fell into a deep sleep and when Adam got back with Kate at about 4.30 I was still fast asleep. I woke feeling as though I was still at the bottom of the pond of afternoon sleep, all muddy and green and groggy.

Today is the day I'm visiting Sally, with my friend, for tea. I have to take eight cartons of cigarettes to get her to the end of December; perhaps I should buy a carton or two extra. The thought of her having smoked her way through all those cigarettes makes me queasy.

I am at that time in my life where I keep feeling sad, all the lost horses, all the lost dogs, all the lost people, the past, the past. I try not to dwell on it all too much, to sink into it. But every now and then, I am struck with it all, my grandparents, their dogs, their houses, my father, my mother, my sister who now lives abroad and her children, and the horses, and all those days and years that have just gone forever.

We can only give you seven cartons
27 November

So on Wednesday I went with Barbara to have tea with my mom. Barbara fetched me, kindly. I'd asked her if we could stop at Shoprite to get the cigarettes. She stayed in the car at Century City and I ran in to get them. I did my time in the queue at the cigarette counter, and when it was my turn, I asked for eight cartons, and the lady gave me eight boxes, "No, I said eight cartons." She had to get a key because the cartons are locked up in a special stockroom. Cigarettes are a form of currency.

She said she could only give me seven cartons. Why was that, I wondered. Do Shoprite want to create a feeling of scarcity around cigarettes for the heavy smokers? Or did they only have seven cartons? Or did they want to be sure to keep some for the other customers? Next time I will ask for twelve and see what happens. Anyhow, I got seven cartons, two plastic bags and R2400 later, with a queue building up behind me, I swung the bags off the counter and walked away, trying to look cool with buying so many cigarettes. My queue-mates looked at me. I could hear their thoughts. Spaza shop? Gosh! Maybe she lives out in the sticks. They were all wondering. I fiercely kept myself from explaining. The whole spree took less than 15 minutes, and we didn't have to pay the R7 for parking. Small mercies.

We picked Barbara's mom up first from her apartment and then went to get mine. I called her from the lobby and she came down to meet us. I felt a little anxious – how would

Barbara see me after meeting my mom? As we were having tea, either Barbara or her mom told me that I look like Sally. Not a thing I like to hear, even though I know it is true. I guess it's because I can't see beyond who she is now. Barbara said she could see that she had been a handsome woman. We had an Appletiser, two teas and a Coke.

My mom didn't make much of an effort, or maybe she couldn't. Barbara, her mom and I kept the conversation going, like the shuttlecock in badminton. Every now and then it did actually fall on the floor and someone had to pick it up and bat again. My mom kept asking Barbara's mom, "Oh, do you live in Laguna Beach?"

"Yes," said Barbara's mom, over and over again, as if she were answering the question for the first time. That was Sally's only contribution to the conversation. She did also once say that something wasn't her cup of tea; I made a joke, "that's not my can of Coke". She smiled but it was more of a grimace.

I envy Barbara her mom. She is 76 and still spry and charming, she drives and comes over for dinner once a week. She is enjoying her life. A discussion ensued about the view of Table Mountain from my mother's apartment. Sally said she liked it. First time I heard of it. She once said, when I asked her if she liked the view of the mountain. "Well I've seen it hundreds of times before." (Turns out she does like it, especially at night.)

I felt as though I had shared an intimate secret with B, taking her to my mother, showing her the source of it all, as it were. I enjoyed the visit and felt almost tender and loving towards my mother. But I was somewhat wiped out by the time I'd got home, fetched Kate from aftercare, landed. I didn't go to the music event I'd planned to go to, the visit had taken all the energy I had for the day. Even the next day I felt like I was running on empty.

Ouroboros
2 December

On my Walk for Life walk this morning I felt awful, as though the slightest provocation might make me burst into tears. I was the person at the very back and didn't feel as though I could go much faster. Something in me struggles against being last. I wanted to cheat even, thought of short cuts. Of course I didn't take any, but I wanted to. I kept telling myself, don't be silly, it is OK, it's not a race.

Had to miss analysis yesterday. Took Kate to the doctor, she has had a sore tummy, been running a temperature for days on and off, and just feeling out of sorts. Now am waiting to hear if she has glandular fever.

My computer isn't connecting to the Internet via our Telkom line, so I'm using my 3G dongle, while I wait for the IT guy to come. Spent hours yesterday talking to different people at Telkom. The last chap had a slightly impatient tone to his voice. He sounded gay, urban Afrikaans. Must be a crap job, frustrating, tedious helping people who don't know their IP from their SP. People like me. But still it is their job. I wonder if he was so gatvol he couldn't pretend any longer.

I feel like getting into bed, curling up with my book and sleeping and dreaming. I wanted to tell my analyst about my snake dream.

It started out with a small wooden snake curled up with a bigger one, a blue snake. Then the blue snake moved. At first the other people in my dream thought it was also wooden and moved only because it was being touched, but I felt sure it was alive, and real. Eventually it became clear it was a real live snake.

Outside there were many snakes; you had to be careful not to stand on them. I saw two snakes, one of which was eating into the back of the first snake. It made me think of the Ouroboros, a snake eating its own tail, even though there were two snakes.

"The Ouroboros is a dramatic symbol for the integration and assimilation of the opposite, i.e. of the shadow," it says in Wikipedia. Which makes me think it was a good dream. An important dream. Ah well, only have to wait another week, and my analyst will help me to understand it.

The details
3 December

Have to pay my mother's levy and an outstanding insurance amount. And her chemist bill. And before I go away, do another shop for Cokes, and ensure she has enough cigarettes for the duration.

In spite of the long to-do list I'm feeling much better today, so is my girl, although she is still not at school because of her glandular fever. Try not to think about it too much.

It's a warm sunny day and my computer is connecting to the internet properly – thanks to a fabulous young techie, a kind, sweet man. Polite, happy to explain things to me. Tracking down all the problems to their very root and then sorting them out.

I spent an hour making paper dolls with Kate this morning. It was fun, although I discovered that my glue, my sharpener and so on had migrated or gone missing, as being in the same vicinity as a small child is wont to make them do. While cutting out and tracing patterns (she has a book with a basic set of dolls and clothes) I imagined myself briefly as a clothes designer. As a girl, I loved clothes and drawing them. The things I love most in gorgeous clothes are the little touches, the contrasts, the little bit of netting at the hem, the details.

That time of year
14 December

December has been so busy; I've hardly touched sides. Now we are about to go on our summer holiday to Nieu Bethesda. I am looking forward to it, but still lots to do. Including visiting my mom tomorrow and taking her a Christmas gift and several cartons of cigarettes.

Kate was ill and then it was the last week of term and Christmas shopping and a big do for work that had to be organised, but all is going well. I'm tired and hot and somewhat enervated tonight, but also full of the sense that a lovely break is in sight.

In the New Year I look forward to planting a veggie garden, and writing every day. And walking most days. Sigh.

It seems to me that others are also frazzled. A young woman was extremely rude to me in Clicks today when I went to fill my prescription for my anti-depressants. I was waiting to be served and was next in line; she went in front of me. I pointed out that I was already waiting. She sneered at me. Stop complaining you bloody old bag, I imagined her saying.

2010

Coughing up
7 January

Back in Cape Town after a good break in Nieu Bethesda. Lovely Christmas with friends, much relaxing, swimming, eating of large, shared, slowly cooked meals. Lots of reading and napping and more swimming.

I've visited my mother already, and taken her seven cartons of cigarettes. Again the thing where the woman behind the counter first tried to give me seven packs of cigarettes, and took a while to realise I wanted seven cartons. I wish I could figure out a way for Sally to smoke less, I worry that she is going to run out of money, which means we her children will have to cough up.

Adam bought an electronic cigarette this week, but I can see it isn't a hit. He says it doesn't feel like a cigarette, it's too heavy. The smoke doesn't smell, which for me is a plus. You don't have to light it; you charge it, and when it's charged you pick it up when you want to have a draw. You have to wait for a short interval before taking your next drag. As none of this appeals to Adam, I can imagine it won't appeal to my mom either.

I also went shopping for clothes for my mom, went to Woollies and bought several pairs of jeans with elasticised waists, and some blouses, and took them to her to try on. Now I'm having some of the jeans hemmed. Size 42 and 44.

I arrived and made her take her clothes off. There she

stood in her panties and her sleeveless vest, trying on different items of clothing. Now to return some of the clothes.

Her microwave doesn't work, it takes up space and acts like window dressing, the make-believe that she cooks for herself sometimes. Every time I see it, I think I must take it away. She was watching the cricket, with four almost empty 2-litre Coke bottles around her feet. Ashtray overflowing. Not a pretty sight.

I forgot to give the carers a gift for taking care of my mom. So will need to transfer some money to Chantel for that. And had to pay an outstanding R790 on her insurance. I wonder if it is worth it, paying insurance for her. I should check her insurance to see if she can't get a cheaper policy.

It's my money
9 January

Had her new trousers altered, now I must take them to her. Maybe tomorrow I'll have her over for lunch. I keep putting it off. It always feels like a hassle to schlep out to Century City to fetch her or see her. Sometimes just the thought of seeing my mother makes me need a long lie-down instead. I suddenly feel exhausted, wiped out, sleepy. I planned to pop out to her yesterday and just didn't make it. OK – will do tomorrow. A resolution.

Eunie, Kate's nanny, altered Sally's pants. She designs and sews some of her own clothes and for others too. A few years ago I gave her my sewing machine. Making your own clothes is a great idea, but not for me.

I'm going to write my mother a letter with a copy to Chantel about her smoking. She is unpleasant and demanding of the carers and people who hand out her cigarettes to her "It's my money," she says, stomping around and swearing at anyone who won't let her have what she wants immediately.

Talking to her in my head: "Yes, Ma it is your money. But you don't have endless money. So you need to work in a budget, like all of us."

The lengths to which I am prepared to go
10 January

Amazing how far I will go to avoid seeing my mother. Today I found when I was about to set off that I had locked my car keys and front door keys and remote for the electric gate in the cubby hole of Adam's car. He was at the Yacht Club – where he works, some of the time. I had to ask a friend to fetch me and take me to the Yacht Club to get my keys out of the cubbyhole. It took about four calls before Adam realised I didn't have to see him or have him leave his keys anywhere. I could take his spare keys. My friend kindly fetched me and we trekked off to fetch the keys.

On the way back we decided to go to the Milnerton Market. I bought two second-hand dark haired Barbie dolls for Kate, for R30. Some dried apricots, a tiny blue bottle, a St Helena ashtray for Adam, as well as a pair of nail clippers (R7 – we are always losing ours). I also bought some stationery for Eunie's adopted son Mandla, some Pritt, HB pencils, a sharpener, the rest I will get at Waltons this week.

I really planned to see my mom, to return the trousers she didn't want/didn't fit, and visit her. But the whole key saga made me think, you know what? you can do this tomorrow, or the next day, or some other day, some other time.

Now I have an hour before I have to leave to fetch a different friend from the airport, she's been on holiday in the Eastern Cape. I have to pick Kate up from her play date and then my friend, and according to Adam I have to make supper. But it's not so easy, he's on diet. And according to our new money regime; there is to be no shopping at Woollies (his rule). So what do I make? Better see what I can defrost. I am uninspired to cook for him and Kate at the best of times. Today it feels ten times more challenging.

Queen of Tarts
11 January

Didn't make it to my mother today. I sent the altered trousers to her by courier. Instead I went stationery shopping with Kate for Mandla's stationery and then we went to tea at the Queen of Tarts. She didn't want to visit my mother either. It's not her idea of fun to visit Sally; there is nothing in it for her. My mother is quiet, and not much that comes from her is fun or even interesting to a child. I will visit her later this week, when Kate is back at school. My mother does not remotely come close to being 'Granny'. She is a sad old lady with not much going for her.

Of course I also worked today, in a sporadic way. But I've got that slightly tired, overwhelmed feeling. Today I'm wishing I didn't have such a complicated and demanding job. Today I wish I could lie in bed and read. Today I wish I could be a child, and not have so many responsibilities.

<u>My</u> marriage
12 January

The new school year starts tomorrow, so today is the last day of the holidays, Kate is going into Grade 2. I still haven't been to see my mom, but I did see my analyst today. Feel much better about things. I get my self into a twist, and lose sight of things, all too easy to do, and she helps me get some perspective.

The thing I came away with today was to think about <u>my</u> marriage rather than my husband's marriage or our marriage. In other words not to predicate how I behave or what I do on what he does or doesn't do, but to behave as I want to, as comes naturally to me. In other words to be generous, sharing, kind and not to operate on a tit for tat basis. I'm going to try it.

Nothing like a cold swim on a hot day
13 January

Cape Town is as hot as hell today, can't think of a better simile. My brain is overheated and so is my body. We went to the beach this afternoon and swam in the Atlantic, the cold side, every time I got into the sea; it felt better, more wonderful. I did wonder about sharks, do they ever venture over to Milnerton side?

I also thought of my mother, how we didn't fetch her and bring her to the beach with us, how she wouldn't have liked it, how I still haven't been to see her since I took her the jeans. How much I was enjoying myself in a low key way with Kate and Adam. Kate made a deep tunnel with a bridge and then kept going to fetch water from the sea to fill up the tunnel/canal. She kept this up for ages. I swam about five times, not for long, but each time I went in, I stayed a bit longer. It was bliss getting so cold and wet, but it didn't take long to heat up again. When Adam had suggested we go to the beach, I wasn't keen, but he cajoled us into the car, and it was the best thing to have done. Cheered us all up. Cooled our frayed tempers and overheated brains.

The beach was full for a weekday afternoon. I love the democracy of the beach, you take your clothes off, the ocean belongs to no-one and to all, we play and swim, all ages, all sizes, and there is space for everyone, always enough space.

Birthday brittle
15 January

Today I went for a walk – 6 kms – and now am at my desk, more focused, although not as focused as I would like to be.

Still haven't been to see my mother, maybe tomorrow afternoon. I'll bake a cake in the morning. My birthday is on Sunday, and I don't want to see my mother on my birthday, that would be a downer. I wonder if the way I feel in January before my birthday doesn't have something to do with my mother, my mother complex. She was 20 years old, probably frightened, overwhelmed and wondering what the hell she was going to do, how she was going to cope with a baby and what it would mean for her life. I guess that is how I feel at this time, a whole year ahead, lots of huge challenges, it's overwhelming. If I see my mother tomorrow, I will ask her to tell me what it was like for her just before I was born. I seem to remember her saying she was hot and her ankles were swollen. And she was in labour for 24 hours. I was born just before midnight.

When I was younger, my birthday was a brittle thing, I expected things to go wrong, to be disappointed. But years of therapy have shifted my expectations, and I am able to give myself the kind of birthday I want, and my feelings of self-worth and confidence aren't undermined, even if it's not celebrated in quite the way I would like by those nearest and dearest. Usually these days I am surprised by getting birthday wishes from people I don't know that well, and surprise calls, and even gifts and treats. I usually do something for my birthday, even if just with my tiny nuclear family. The three of us.

I love celebrating Kate's birthday and this has also been healing for me, to give her the kind of attention and love I would have liked as a child. A cake, a party, presents, lots of hugs and kisses. The little girl inside me also enjoys the birthday celebrations. Kate takes for granted that she will have a lovely birthday and doesn't have a clue what 'birthday brittle' is.

Sentient beings

19 January

My birthday was lovely, no birthday brittle. Lots of fun and love and the pleasure of friends and family. Yummy food, sweet cards, lots of books, and I even got to choose a book as an extra present, as one of the books I got I had already read. Champagne, pound cake (which I made myself). Just had a slice for breakfast with a glass of milk.

But not my mother, still have to go and see her. Maybe this week. Oh dear, I am a dreadful procrastinator.

Kate is so sweet and celebrates my age, 48, with sweetness, no sense that one might not wish to be 48. Well the thing is I am actually OK with 48. Good to feel that too.

Busy reading Diana Athill's collected memoirs, inspiring. It is possible to have a rich, fulfilling, happy old age. I already enjoy the confidence I feel, the stronger sense of self worth, and not being plagued with self-doubt like I used to be.

The odd feeling of being a little ill has lifted; the sore arms, the achiness, the depression. I feel full and raring to go. Just trying to sort out aftercare for Kate. She goes to a school that doesn't have it. Not easy, and until the end of January, school is finishing at 12. Hardly any time at all.

Strange dream this morning, of being on holiday at a hotel by the sea. Fishing boats came right close to shore and caught some large fish, and a shark, and flung them into the hold. I saw that the fish were sentient beings and that being caught and flung into the hold was painful and traumatic. Shortly after that I saw hotel staff cutting up a huge fish into steaks for lunch for the guests. Right then and there in my dream I decided to be a vegetarian.

Although it was clear in the dream, in waking life such a decision isn't so clear-cut at all. It seems to me that we are an awfully cruel species. The shark was caught just for the hell of it. Or maybe it was because a shark attacked and killed a man at Fish Hoek beach last week. A punishment for its species.

Remembering agapanthus
24 January

Finally put off procrastinating and visited my mom today. I woke up feeling full of energy and happy. Lovely day in Cape Town. Started by taking bricks away from one of the beds in my garden. Adam likes the garden to be neat and tidy and having bricked borders works for him. Not for me. I did that for a bit, but got distracted by the hot water leaking from the geyser overflow from the bathroom behind the 'granny flat' which houses our offices.

I felt good enough to call my mother and invite her for lunch even though it meant a drive to Century City. She was keen. I also did the long outstanding chore of returning the clothes that didn't fit her. My to-do list is being ticked off. My car was serviced on Friday and I breathed a sigh of relief when I discovered my two front tyres were worn down to the canvas. Now I've got a serviced car and two new tyres.

Drove out to fetch my mother, gorgeous day, the road works on the M5 and Koeberg interchange are impressive, one of these days it's going to be a spaghetti flyover, hope it prevents the backed up traffic that often happens on that road. No backups today. Smooth driving. Ratanga Junction was open.

I made a delicious chicken stir-fry for lunch. Lunch was pleasant enough, but not much chatting. My mother isn't much of a conversationalist, nor is Adam. Kate only likes chatting when others are. I made a valiant effort, but also didn't try too hard. After lunch Kate went to swim at a friend's house. Her dad took her.

I sat with Sally in the lounge. We went over some familiar territory:

Did I tell you that Sidney has died?

Yes, Ma.

How old is Perry? (our dog)

He's just over three.

Where is your friend, Graeme?

He's in the States.

Oh and his partner?

He doesn't have one at present.

Did I tell you that Carol died?

Yes, you did.

How long have you been married now?

It will be ten years this year. (Ten years, time flies.)

Have you heard from Gerry lately?

Yes, we email about once a week.

How is she? Where does she live again?

and so on...

On the way back to her place she surprised me,

"Agapanthus," she said, referring to the flowers all along Century Boulevard. On the way to my house I'd told her, "I can never remember the name of those flowers."

The still dark place
27 January

For three days I've had a headache. Migraines make me feel I'm like my mother, who was also a chronic headache sufferer. They are debilitating. I feel this pressure closing in on me, forcing me to collapse onto my bed, a pillow over my head, to keep out the light. Sleeping, aware of the pain, feeling pushed, pushed into a ball, small, curled up, the pain there, pressing, oppressing.

I'm a little better now, it's lifted; still there in the distance, but feels as though it has left town. Although it could come back, hasn't got far enough away for me to be sure that it's gone.

I feel like a junkie when I buy painkillers. I think of how my mother abused painkillers and other over-the-counter meds. Went into a pharmacy last night, in Rondebosch and asked the pharmacist for something that would help for a sore neck and shoulders and headache that had hung around for two days, not budging.

"Have you already taken something?"

'Yes, Myprodol."

"OK, let's give you something with a bit of a muscle relaxant in it too."

"OK" I say humbly. He gives me a box of Norflex. They

work, but not altogether, I've had three doses now, one last night, one this morning, and one at about 4. A dose is two tablets. My mouth is dry.

Would love to have a glass of wine, but won't – wine doesn't mix with headaches very well. Lots of water, tea, sleep, rest. Then perhaps it will go.

Headaches put me in mind of my mother complex. They used to affect me even more severely and frequently than now. I would cower before them, crumple into a heap. Disappear into a still, dark place, with the headache standing guard at the cave's entrance. If I moved or returned from the depths, the pain would pounce and pound at me.

Frequently the headaches, migraines really, would be accompanied by nausea, vomiting, sweats, feeling trembly. But there is nothing like the calm clarity after a migraine. An altered sense of the world. A new place, a place of beauty and a place that is far away from and doesn't include pain.

Migraines force me to obey, stop, let go. Until they are over. Submit to the episode. The more I resist the more painful it becomes, and the longer it takes to recede. Migraines force me to remember that I am not a machine, that I am limited, and that only so much is possible.

Bee cream
30 January

Something I wrote a couple of nights ago disappeared in the way that dreams do when you wake, you can only vaguely remember what it was about.

Today I'm sore from a fall I had yesterday morning, less sore than yesterday, but the graze on the middle finger of my left hand is slightly infected. I've put some antiseptic cream on it, and a kiddies safari plaster. I love kiddies' plasters, they are so satisfying to use, make it seem as though a sore is kind of fun. Bit like getting a kiss on the sore place.

When Kate was littler I used to buy boxes of Barney and dinosaur plasters just for her to play with, amazing the amount of pleasure a box of plasters can provide. Of course there was often not a plaster when one was needed, but still. It was the kind of thing we weren't allowed to do when I was a child, to waste or play with plasters. I think the 1960s were still too close to the war and the period of rationing in which my mother grew up.

'Bee cream' is our resource for most minor scratches and skin ailments. It is a way of tending to the feeling of being hurt in a safe and gentle way. Kate loves bee cream. She likes the smell and she's seen that it works. My first analyst once explained to me that if she hurt or injured herself, it was important to her to tend to her hurt, to pay it attention and do something gentle to herself. I guess I must have imbibed that notion; I like to tend to Kate. Once she hurt her knee running to meet me. I'd been out all day. She cried and we cleaned her knee and kissed and put bee cream on it and then we lay on my bed for a bit together and cuddled. She said to me, "I just want a few minutes of undivided attention from you, Mommy". We snuggled a bit longer and then she got up and went to play with her friend in the lounge.

I fell yesterday, the first day of my period, after several

days of a bad headache that came and went. I didn't feel like going for my aerobic walk, but forced myself to go, I was afraid I was losing motivation for exercise. While I was driving I thought of telling Naomi that I wanted to walk around the field. But I didn't do that. Instead of taking it easy and being kind to myself, I went off for the road walk, tried to keep up with two other women, and hit my head on a concrete garden wall as I fell.

Guardian angels
2 February

Just ordered my mother's Cokes online from Pick n Pay, as well as the *You* magazine, and various other small items. Comes to over R1000. Can't believe how much money my mother wastes. As I write this I think just because she makes choices that I wouldn't make, does it mean she is wasteful? I hear how judgmental I am. What do I waste money on? Let me think. It's not so easy to see how I waste. Yesterday I bought ice cream and ate ice cream for supper. I don't normally do things like that, but as I felt crap, I let myself have something cold, soft and sweet for supper. Kate had a sore tooth, a molar is coming through, she also had an odd supper, yoghurt and honey and bacon. In two courses. The bacon separately.

I went to Walk for Life today, and feel much better for walking the 5 kms. Walked with two women I have become friendly with – I feel safe walking with them. One of my walking companions is hyper aware of cars and safety, a guardian angel. She walks about 200 kms a month, enormously inspiring. I am pleased with myself for going today, especially as I felt really wonky and out of sorts all weekend.

One of those days
4 February

One of those days, no electricity at home; the sub-station is being repaired. I lost my keys before taking the girls to school. Took spares, but they don't have house keys attached. Later took Kate to the dentist, she has to go once a month for a while, her teeth need to be monitored, her enamel isn't developing the way it should. Her teeth are vulnerable to plaque and bacterial deterioration because of all the antibiotics she had as a prem baby. Our dentist really likes Kate and is interested in her and kind to her.

My day was one of rushing and not being centred. I had a little row with Adam before bed. He was feeling down today about money and the long-term prospects of earning a living. Tough for us that we are both self-employed. Some of our work is freelance, so it requires a certain determination and positive thinking – not always easy. Our rows usually happen when one of us is in a funk. We seem to find it hard to be there for the other when we are needed.

A bright spot in my day, went to check out new phones, and have decided to get a Blackberry, Adam's phone is due for an upgrade now while mine is only in October. I lost my good phone into a lei water canal in Nieu Bethesda a couple of months after getting it. I want a phone I can use for email, Facebook, Twitter and taking photos.

Tomorrow I will drop off my mom's cigarettes when I go to my accountant in Montagu Gardens.

Same water, different bridges
7 February

Got the Blackberry. And I'm figuring it out and enjoying it, I've become more adept at using techie gadgets than I was when I got my first cellphone about 10 years ago. I wasn't an early adopter.

Took cigarettes to my mom on Thursday. Just dropped them off, didn't want to stay, had things to do. A good meeting with my accountant. Feel optimistic about my prospects.

Saw my brother Sean for the first time in a long while. He popped in. "I just can't visit her at that place. It's too depressing. She just sits there, day after day, all she does is smoke, drink Coke, and watch TV. No man." I didn't know what to say. It depresses me too, but I don't feel able to ditch her. Nice to see my brother though, there is so much water under the bridge, some of the same water, maybe different bridges.

Adam came home with a lot of raspberries and blackberries; I'm going to make a berry crumble for dessert for supper tonight. Kate has gone to a party this afternoon. It's been a quiet, very Sundayish day, cabin feverish. Something lifeless about the day. I had a nap even though I slept well last night. Catching up on stuff, reading, replying. Making times. The schedule for next week.

Dreaming of snakes

Last night had another powerful snake dream. I was putting Kate to bed, not here at home, but in a holiday bungalow. The room was darkish, nighttime; she was in bed under a duvet. The bed wasn't right up against the wall or window and as I was about to sit down on it, I saw a snake slither into the room, across the wooden floor. A big snake, red with black markings and a yellow face, a frightening snake. I called Adam and he came in and reached down and picked the snake up, he held it in such a way that it couldn't bite him. He had to grapple with it a bit first. I was rooted to the spot, immobilised in that way that happens in dreams. While he was trying to pick the snake up, I was full of fear, part of me wanted the snake to bite him and kill him and the other part was afraid that it would. He managed to dispose of the snake, took it out of the room and put it outside, far away. I woke up my heart pounding.

In waking life I am angry with him because he is making it hard (to put it mildly) for me to give Kate a kitten. I really want her to have a cat, and I think she would enjoy one. As an only child, I think it would be good for her to have an animal familiar. A cat would offer her a place outside of the tightness of our tiny nuclear family, a place in which she and the cat can have another sort of relationship. I was thinking of getting us an Abyssinian crossbreed kitten. An old friend of mine has some that will be ready to go to their new homes in a few weeks. Sometimes marriage feels like the hardest possible way to live.

Romance and the Middle-Aged Woman
2 March

Last night I dreamt about an old lover, my first real love. So long ago, yet he remains a firm favourite in my dream life. I'd been to see *A Single Man* – a romantic movie steeped in loss and memories. Of course Colin Firth is adorable in the movie, his face lights up with his shy, dimpled, soulful smile. The movie must have prompted my dreamer into remembering my first love. In the dream we were at university – he had left me the way he did in real life, and was with the woman he is now married to and has been for 20 years. In the dream, he kept Saturday afternoons for me, and we would have these dates. We would hang out, go for walks, cuddle, have sex, and all the while it made me feel awful, because it was all so limited and he wasn't 'mine'. Self torture. It rained a lot in the dream. We went for walks in the rain, or cowered indoors, or went up to my res room and lay about and touched each other's bodies.

Now onto my daytime torture, ha-ha. I did my mother's shopping on Sunday after a lovely day out with old friends and family. Lunch at Jonkershuis under the old trees, drinking delicious wine and laughing and feeling happy. As good as it gets. Sally called me in the morning to say she had run out of Cokes, which I already knew would happen. I was supposed to have ordered them, but hadn't. I quickly did so on Sunday evening as well as her other stuff, the toilet paper and toothpaste. Still have to do the cigarettes.

I had this insight, a sad one, although it didn't pierce my heart as much as the movie or my dreams; I realised my mother was much more connected to her cigarettes and Coke than she is to me. Her own needs and addictions come first in her life, absolutely and totally. Now it is even more extreme, as I am the conduit, the buzzer that her inner hamster presses. Nothing romantic or redeeming about that. Except it is real and I'm seeing without illusions.

No rest for the wicked
3 March

Oh damn, I forgot to buy my mother cigarettes; not being able to buy them online is killing me. I will have to go out, and it is unbearably hot. Oh well. No rest for the wicked. I was in Rondebosch at the Pick n Pay Centre where I could have easily bought cigarettes. My brain must have been addled by the heat. Too many things on my to-do list today.

Sometimes wish I had a robot I could summon when I need things done and could say, "Look here you are, off you go, please buy seven cartons of Rothmans thirties, the blue pack, and then take them over to Century City, would you? There's a dear."

Where there's smoke
11 March

I got Adam to buy the cigarettes, he bought the wrong brand, but there has been no complaint. He bought Peter Stuyvesant, and my mother smokes Rothmans. But she isn't as brand loyal as all that. She smokes Adam's Marlboros or Camels if she runs out when she visits us. He has an odd habit; he buys filter tip cigarettes and then breaks the filters off. I don't get it, nor do I try to. Cigarette smoking is an arcane practice as far as I am concerned. If I see smoke or fire, I don't try to get closer and inhale. Am I missing something?

I planned to have my mother over on Sunday, but it was so hot here, almost 40 degrees. So after a swim at Milnerton, I didn't want to emerge from the house. Luckily I hadn't told her. I only ever let her know just before I plan to fetch her, perhaps an hour or two at most; I know about my fluctuating energy levels. Maybe this weekend. Except it is the Argus. Bicycles everywhere and roads closed.

My sister is coming out from the States for a week, would be nice to do a family thing, like go to Buitenverwachting for a picnic or something. It looks lovely, haven't been there, but it's been recommended and it looks perfect on the website. It would be nice for all of us – my mother and all her children and their spouses, and grandchildren, it would be the first time we will have been together as a family for a long time.

Teeth

18 March

While driving Kate and her classmate (our lift club) to school yesterday morning, I got a call from a sister at the LRR. Apparently some of Sally's teeth have fallen out. How odd. So I made a dentist's appointment and today she went. I had to fill in a 4-page form with her details and give the dentist's assistant my credit card details. Today I get a call from the dentist himself. He was horrified at my mother's teeth. It appears she hasn't been brushing her teeth. Her mouth is full of plaque, caries, bacteria and various other oral horrors. He was cross with the LRR as they are supposed to care for her and he feels they are being negligent in their care. Am I also being negligent? I guess it is not enough to just have her in a so-called Luxury Retirement Resort, the High Care Centre. What exactly does High Care mean, I wonder?

It is also the Coke. He is going to have to take some more teeth out, and make a denture for her upper teeth. Oh dear. I feel guilty. I will have to make more of an effort somehow.

The dentist was appalled to hear that she only drinks Coke and no other liquids. Not a good prognosis. But in many other ways she is healthy. I will see her on Sunday this week. Will have to see her. I wanted to go to the Kirstenbosch plant sale. But one big thing on a Sunday is enough.

I couriered cigarettes over to her. Pick n Pay in Rondebosch didn't have any Rothmans 30s cartons. So I bought Peter Stuyvesant again, and some Rothmans 20s cartons and 10 loose packs of Rothmans 30s. I had to ask my friend if I could have the courier fetch them from her, as I had an all morning meeting on Wednesday.

I have arranged the family picnic.

Non-compliance
25 March

Just got a call from the sister at the LRR saying my mother needs to see her psychiatrist. She has become non-compliant about taking her meds. She hides them, flushes them down the loo, throws them down the lift shaft, and various other tactics to avoid taking them. The psychiatrist I went to see at Milnerton Mediclinic hasn't followed up. Damn. Last week her teeth. This week her madness. Again. I phoned to ask my GP to find out if she can recommend a psychiatrist in the Milnerton area. Waiting to hear.

My mother is like a difficult, bad child. I was telling my sister and brother on Sunday how she had cut off the sleeves and legs of her pajamas with a pair of nail scissors. They were pretty cotton summer pajamas. I got a call from her yesterday, "Colleen, I need toilet paper." Phoned Chantel to ask her to provide.

The lawn turns to sand
20 April

School holidays, Kate is watching *The Sound of Music* over and over again. Adam is working on his boat outside in the driveway. The lawn turns to sand. We have a new kitten,

Jessy. She is playful, but also scratches and bites. She romps and leaps; her eyes bright and alert, curious.

World Cup Football
10 June

The World Cup starts tomorrow. We don't have tickets to any games, but are planning to go to the Fan Park in town at the Grand Parade tomorrow.

Been working very hard for ages, and on Monday week – I am taking a week off work, will go with Kate to Grahamstown to stay with a friend. Looking forward to that.

My mother's behaviour has deteriorated since I last wrote; the psychiatrist and nursing staff are wondering what to do with her.

No landmarks
6 July

Grahamstown. I spent the day at the farm, where I lived for five years. It's on the Highlands Road on the way towards Alicedale. Kate was at the Children's Festival all day. Driving out to the farm on the rutted dirt road, I remembered a drive home to the farm, in the fog, I hadn't been living there long, just a few months. The fog disoriented me so, I thought I might drive off the road, miss the turn off, get lost. I couldn't hear or see anything. There were no landmarks, no reference points.

Sixty-nine
12 July

Visited my mother yesterday, I got there just as they were finishing lunch. She sits at a table in the far corner with some other ladies, who are ten if not twenty years older than she is. I took her roses (from the nearby Woollies) and a carton of cigarettes, my brother had organised them from a mate of his who got them cheap from duty free. We went up to her apartment and I trimmed the stalks then arranged the roses in a vase. She likes having flowers. She was watching Jeremy Clarkson in Tokyo driving on the extraordinary freeways, racing two friends who were using public transport. Every now and then she would turn away from the TV and look at the roses, and say, "Pretty, aren't they?"

Eventually I broached the subject of her will. I'd been dreading the will conversation for many months. But she was calm about it, and said that she had made a will with my father, along the same lines. I explained that a new will would make things administratively easier for all concerned (especially me, I was thinking) when the time came. She was very easy-going about it. Made me realise that sometimes I make mountains out of molehills. Or maybe she was just in a good space. Taking her meds.

She's had her hair cut recently and looked much better than she does when her hair is longer, wild and bushy, makes her look like a crazy frump. She was almost beautiful again. She still has good bone structure and very blue eyes. When I left, I popped into the nurses' station to alert them to her chesty cough.

It's her birthday on Friday, she'll be 69. I'm planning to have my brothers and their families over for lunch on Sunday. It is much more fun when they are all here, more lively, and she likes it too.

The problem of buying cigarettes
28 July

I took Sally her new will to sign, she'd been cooperative and I got my attorney to draft it. She signed in front of two of the women at reception. Now I have it signed and in my bag, and will get it off to my attorney for safe-keeping tomorrow.

I also bought her shoes and cigarettes. In Pick n Pay I was told variously that they only had one carton of Rothmans 30s King-size and that they can only sell one carton per customer. The helpful assistant suggested that if I need to buy such large quantities of cigarettes I should consider getting them from the wholesaler. "Yes please," I said. "Tell me how to buy from the wholesaler." A more managerial chap appeared on the scene, was very polite and wanted to find a solution. We eventually decided that I could pay by EFT two days before I need the cigarettes for my mom. He will then deliver them to her. After months and months of trying to find a way of getting cigarettes to her, a way has finally opened.

I was so annoyed before getting to the solution that I nearly lost it. I still feel weak-armed, shaky and exhausted. Not just from this though. I've bought a tonic rich in

Vitamin B. Hope it helps.

My mom went to a podiatrist last week, and her feet look good, no scaly dry skin and calluses. Her toenails are neat and her skin looks soft and tender. I'm proud. But also asking myself why did it take me so long to get her there? Now she has new shoes too.

Non-smoking building throughout
19 November

Yesterday I received a letter from the LRR management who informed me that my mother may no longer smoke in her apartment. Apparently the LRR is now a non-smoking building throughout.

Huge sigh. There is always something else to work out. Just when I'd sorted out the whole cigarette delivery system with Pick n Pay. The system was slightly rocky at first, but has stabilised.

Here's the thing. We wouldn't have bought an apartment for my mother at the LRR if we knew that they were going to become a non-smoking building. I don't know how we are going to manage this. I phoned our attorney and he has suggested that I get mediation via an advocate who works in the same building as him. He cautioned against getting too heavy with the LRR and to rather try and find a way to sort things out by talking.

Dealing with my mother, or even thinking about dealing with her, tires me. Sometimes it feels like a full-time job, managing her and her needs. Just to list some of what I have done for her in the last while: I bought her some new sandals; beach slip-ons with a single broad strap across the foot. I saw them in her cupboard the other day. She has never worn them. The shoes she wears every day are very grubby and are going to fall off her feet one of these days. Shopping for shoes for Sally means going to a shoe shop, buying three pairs, taking them to her to try on, her choosing a pair, and then me going back to return the other two pairs.

I also bought her panties. I'd got a slightly frantic call, in fact four calls from her and one from the sister, telling me she had no panties. I began to wonder what she had done with them. She has a history of throwing things away. A history of destructive behaviour. Breaking things too. I bought her four packs of five XL cotton briefs from the Woollies in Pinelands. Also a nightie, some t-shirts, a pair of cotton pajama pants that you can wear with a T-shirt. And a pretty blue cotton blouse from Robelle, the ladies outfitters in Pinelands at the Howard Centre. They cater for older and larger women.

Oh and I also had to deal with a short period where she wanted to smoke 90 cigarettes a day, so to have an extra pack of 30s a day over and above her 'normal' 60 a day. Beats me how someone smokes that much. I got the psychiatrist to see her and tell her to smoke only 60, "doctor's orders" which she will listen to more than anything said by me, or anyone at the LRR.

2011

"Mom is completely non-compliant you know"
22 May

I haven't written for ages, but have been busy with both my mother's madness and mine, and many other things besides.

Last week I was asked to attend a meeting at the LRR. My brother Mike came along. We squashed into a small office – me, my brother, the cheerful and sweet OT, the head of nursing, and the sister who runs the Alzheimer's Unit, Sister Burger.

Seemed like they wanted to tell us how much of a handful and a nightmare Sally is. "Mom is completely non-compliant you know," Sister Burger says.

I'm not sure what they want us to do, but we go and see her after the meeting to try and convey to her what has been conveyed to us. Her small apartment looks awful. The beach-sand-coloured fitted carpet is blackish, fading to dark grey, she must drop ash all the way to her bed and then to the bathroom. She has a plastic mat in front of her LazyBoy chair, so under the mat it is not quite as dark grey as the rest of the carpet. Chantel had asked me to provide the mat. Sally hates it.

Her beautiful embroidered curtains are yellowy from the nicotine, and have burn marks in them here and there. Her sofa has dark ring marks on it, from Coke glasses put down.

"I'm not having my hair cut. I can't stand that bloody bitch," she says of the hairdresser. She repeated a number of times that she had kept her promise to shower every day and wash her hair every day. We know this is not true, but that is what she says. Unless we put a webcam in her apartment, how can we prove it to her? And then the thought of watching her on a webcam. And even if we did prove to her that she doesn't shower enough, it wouldn't be proof enough.

They had told us at the LRR meeting that she was abusive, shouts and swears at the carers, and even hit one the other day. Sister Burger says that it is her bipolar that makes her like this. Later on in the meeting Sister Burger says, "We are not a facility for the mentally ill."

Where is this going? Will she have to be moved to Valkenburg? I suspect the state facilities won't want her anyway, as she has resources to pay her own way.

I tell her that unless she becomes more compliant and does not attack the carers, she might have to be moved to Valkenburg. "What, am I mad?" she asks.

We mention that Sister Burger says she doesn't take her meds properly. "Why do I have to take eight different kinds of pills anyway?" she asks, a petulant note in her voice. She is sitting slumped in her LazyBoy, looking down at the floor, as though we her adult children are school principals, and she has been summoned to the principal's office against her will.

According to Sister Burger, she hides her meds, pretends to take them. "Then she throws them out of the window, down the lift shaft. We find them all over the place." How do they know that they are her meds, I wonder? But I know they are hers.

It is impossible to argue with Sally, to persuade her. To

make her admit to what she does and does not do. To take responsibility. After all that is why she is there, living at the LRR, rather than on her own. "Please don't flush your panties down the loo." This is another complaint that the LRR has against her. They have had to call in plumbers on several occasions because of panties blocking the toilet.

"It was an accident," she says, "I didn't do it on purpose." I try to picture how she could have accidently dropped a pair of panties in the loo.

"Just rinse them out," I suggest, "and then pop them into your wash basket."

"I do rinse them out and then hang them to dry in the shower."

I feel defeated and tired and yet comforted by my brother as we drive back home. My mother's parting shot to us was, "Thanks for coming, even though it wasn't very pleasant."

This was on Monday. Today is Sunday. All week I've been tired, irritable and overwhelmed. It's been one of the hardest challenges of my whole life, managing my mother in her decline. Having to make decisions for her. Hearing from her carers how impossible she is.

Seeing, not seeing
24 May

On Thursday I have to take my mother to see an ophthalmologist, she has to have her cataracts removed. I organise a lift home from ballet for Kate, as I won't be back in time to fetch her.

Kate's birthday is on Monday, and her party the following Saturday. She has had a party every birthday and takes it for granted. She loves her party and takes months to plan the details. I love giving her a party. This week I need to order her cake, source large sheets of newsprint, glue, scissors, paints, brushes, magazines to cut up. The activity this year is to make life-size body maps and to decorate and paint them.

I saw my analyst today and told her of the awful meeting with the LRR of last week, and how it left me feeling drained. And how I found Adam much more annoying than usual. Felt worn down and worn out.

On Tuesday next week I have to see my mother's psychiatrist before he sees her. He's going to assess her to decide on her placement. I suspect that the LRR wants to edge her to frail care or out of the facility altogether.

Tomorrow I am going to shop for Kate's birthday. Money is a little tight, so I will have to be imaginative. I had to buy her some new school clothes today. She's growing fast, and will be a tall girl. Tonight when she was eating her supper, picking bits of vegetables out of the bolognaise sauce, I thought I should take a picture to show her when she is older, she may not remember how much she detested vegetables in any size, shape or form.

Now to sleep. It is not late, but I am tired. We still have mosquitoes in spite of the rains and the cold. Isn't there a period when the mosquitoes disappear?

This is not about you

Last night I dreamed of my old lover, the one who right through my adult life continues to star in my dreams. In the dream I want him, want him to want me; want, desire, long for, something I can never have, and yet am not afraid to want. I feel alive this morning, vibrating with desire, longing and yet calm.

In my Facebook inbox a message from another man from long ago, inviting me to lunch with him today. I would have liked to see him. Kate has a bad cold and it seems to me she should not go to school today. So I say to him, "No, not today, but do ask me again." I am pleased by the prospect that I could have had lunch today with a man who looks at me intently and smiles and laughs easily. A man who when he was telling me about his boy, now in matric, cradles his arms and looks down at the baby boy he can see there in his arms. There is much water under the bridge between us, but that water has long since reached the sea.

There is still a charge between us, a frisson. How wonderful to feel that again, after all this time, when it seems to me at times that my sexual body has gone to sleep or moved to a different neighbourhood, a neighbourhood of sexual silence, of gardening, washing the dishes, making sandwiches for school, and working at the table, reading quietly in the sun on my bed on Saturday afternoon.

So today I find that I am still alive in all sorts

of ways I had forgotten about. But the difference between who I am now and who I was then is that I no longer feel the need to act impulsively. I sit here at my keyboard, and feel alive and tingling.

I am letting go of something. Something that is trapped in the frozen life sapping wastes of my mother. The mother complex. Today I am quietly happy. Alive. Full of longing and desire. Quietly.

Cataracts
31 May

Yesterday my mother had the cataract removed from her left eye. I took her to the hospital, had to leave home at 7.30 and got her there just in time at 8.45. The road was slick and sluggish with traffic and road works. As I drove I was impressed with the indigenous plantings along the side of the West Coast road. With the new MyCiti bus service lanes and bus stops, it all looks very 21st century. I wasn't in a great mood; being around my mother does that to me. She was clearly anxious and kept asking who was going to fetch her afterwards. I'd organised for the driver of the LRR and a carer to fetch her, as she was going to be at the hospital for hours.

My mother had this tense, cross, suspicious look on her face and she kept looking sideways and upwards at the nurse who was writing down her details and taking her blood pressure and so on. She had to take her clothes off, but could keep her "broeks" on (her word). She complained about the surgical gown as she put it on. There was her body, uncared for, skin dry on her back and all the scars from her many surgeries. She looked like an old package that has been torn open, wrapped and rewrapped again and again.

She walks slowly and finds it hard to get up from a chair by herself. She has become noticeably frailer. She lied to the nurse about how much she smokes, she told the nurse 20 a day.

"No, mom," I said, "it is two packs of 30."

"Oh," she says, "I thought it was only 20. Sometimes Chantel only gives me 20."

No, mom, she doesn't, I say to myself.

Today I have to see my mom's psychiatrist again. And I have had to organise for her to go back to see the ophthalmologist on Wednesday. I have found a good taxi service; I think when I have her over for lunch, I might use them. I still need to do her Pick n Pay shop today for Cokes and toilet paper, soap, toothpaste and so on.

I need toilet paper
7 June

My mother phones me. "Colleen, please I need toilet paper."

"But I bought some for you last week, I will phone downstairs and see what the story is."

"Yes, please do that."

I phone reception and the nice man downstairs sends a carer up to my mother's apartment. She finds the toilet paper in the kitchen cupboard, not piled up on the bathroom floor as it usually is.

My mother phones me to tell me this. "Why the bloody hell is it in the kitchen? I need it in the bathroom."

I call the man at Pick n Pay; he knows what I want from him. Cigarettes, lots of them. Seven cartons. He will text me the amount that I must pay by EFT.

Last week I also saw my mother's psychiatrist, a pre-briefing before he sees her and assesses her, to determine whether she is OK in assisted living or whether she should be moved to frail care, or what. If it is frail care, that will be the last move before the final one.

My friend got me to agree to throw away my comfiest jersey, because really it is a very ugly jersey, shlumpy is not even the word to describe it. I know it is the right thing to do, and I am wearing it for the last time tonight. I will put it in a bag and leave it out for the garbage bin pickers on Friday; it might be of some use to someone. Before it got baggy and frayed, it had belonged to my late mother in law.

Under the radar

I'm not sure if it is because of the breakdown of family/families or my own inadequate mother or the early 21st century, but I often find myself with not quite enough help with Kate. But I do also realise I am lucky. I have mobilised all kinds of help and probably could ask for more. It is not easy for me to ask though.

This morning at 6.00 I got a Please Call Me from Eunie, "uMandla is sick," she said. Mandla is her cousin's child; she has taken him on as his legal guardian. So she can't come in today.

Mostly I have Saturday mornings off. This morning Kate and I have read the whole of *Five Have Plenty of Fun*. Kate has just fallen in love with Enid Blyton. I've washed the dishes, while she is reading, slightly crossly to herself, *Five Go Off in a Caravan*. I snuck off to my laptop, to play Word Twist. I feel as though I am stealing time, sneaking off, trying to do things under the radar. Any minute now, I expect Kate to come marching in here. She will tell me off and insist I go and read more with her.

After three hours of high-level interaction, I just want a tiny little window of being left alone. I realise I am a little annoyed with Eunie, but also how irrational this is. She works four half days and usually a full day on Saturday, till 4. We pay her wages equivalent to full time. I'm trying not to sound as though I am moaning, just documenting the warp and weft of my life. I never feel entitled to complain about Eunie. Her life is so much harder in every way.

Kate adores Eunie and was disappointed that she wasn't coming in today. Eunie knows how to play with children, she plays with Kate all day on Saturday, and sometimes she brings Mandla, who is just a few months older than Kate. I find playing quite a strain, and am only able to keep at it for shortish periods of time. I guess I find it hard to relax, to allow the rules of a game that Kate has made up to govern my being. I feel slightly restless, impatient and try not to show it.

My favourite games are when I am allowed to do something else, like weed the garden while she weaves the story of the game around me, when I'm only required to be present physically and to agree or sympathise or answer simple questions now and then, while Kate runs up and down the garden, pretending we are horses or dinosaurs and tells the story of the dangers and threats we are under. She builds little gardens and parks and play spaces for the game and the characters. My being there makes it realer for her somehow. I'm not sure what value I add to these games, but if there are no other children or no Eunie, then my presence is definitely required.

The Big Walk
9 November

Loved the Big Walk yesterday. It was a joyful democratic experience of Cape Town, thousands of walkers, from all walks of life (as it were). All of us there in the soft rain, ready to walk the 5 kms. The route was along familiar roads, ones I drive repeatedly. Yet on foot, as part of a human river pulsing forward, they felt different. Main Road, Newlands, Rondebosch, Rosebank, Mowbray and Obs. The delicious coffee shop next to Folio Books in Newlands, where I was tempted to stop. The Jehovah's Witness congregation leaving their small church as we walked past. At Pick n Pay in Rondebosch, I saw two girls with numbers on their chests dash off up the escalators. (To where? To do what?) The 'indigenous' hair salons that offer hair extensions, the fast food joints. The LifeLine Charity Shop.

I relished coming down the off-ramp on foot, barricaded off, the loud roar and swish of cars passing in the rain, and us, people on foot reclaiming a space normally reserved for cars. It took me 66 minutes to get all the way to the finish at St George's School; we entered the school grounds past Kate's old aftercare. Loud music and radio jocks encouraging us in that brash, jokey way. I was drenched, feet soggy and socks squelchy, my anorak no longer keeping the rain out. I took my medal and free Coke and walked slowly to my friend's house. She lives in the same road as St George's. Hot shower, coffee, dry clothes and a kind lift home.

Kate was thrilled by my Big Walk experience and took the medal to school for Show and Tell.

The Sugar Plum Fairy and the Good Enough Mother
10 November

I adored seeing *The Nutcracker* on Saturday afternoon. Kate dressed up. The weather wild and wintry. The Baxter was full, children of all ages, and mothers and fathers. We sank into our seats; by the time I booked there were only expensive seats left, so we sat close to the front.

The performance satisfied me in so many ways: the darkness, the comfortable chairs, and my daughter next to me. Seeing the familiar story made strange and new, in fact the producers changed the story quite a lot. Drosselmeyer (the family friend who brings gifts) and the Sugar Plum Fairy were made into one character, played by a very tall, beautiful black woman who had the most extraordinary presence. She embodied the good mother, one who sees, one who holds Clara (the little girl who is the main character) in her awareness and tends to her, guards her, and shows her the world. Leads her into dreams, imagination, and unexpected magic.

The story was also changed in that the nutcracker was a drum. The changes gave the ballet African touches. I was very impressed with the dancing, especially the showcase dancing in the last act. The costumes were simple and lovely, so were the sets and the music (although in the last scene the recording they were using was a little scratchy).

Music, dancing, spectacle, beauty, dreamy realm of the imagination; the ballet is all of that.

On Fire
25 November

I've had to go to the LRR – Sally set fire to her apartment accidentally, she'd emptied her ashtray into the bin, and in it there was a stompie that was still smoldering. She has to be housed somewhere else in the building while her small apartment is refurbished.

Who will pay for what
26 November

There is a dispute with the insurance company about who will pay for what. The LRR doesn't want to claim from their insurance; they are meant to be a non-smoking building. A fire like this one will up the premiums and will lead to their insurers asking questions they don't want asked. My mother's insurers say that she pays a levy, which they think should cover damage to the building. I ask, "What about the public liability she pays for?"

Someone will have to pay. It will probably be my mother. Or me on her behalf.

She has been relocated to the frail care section in the interim, a double room. She has become more sociable, probably because she spends time downstairs now. I had to go there yesterday and take her new underwear. She had run out. She still throws her underwear away if it gets soiled.

Not the Three Bears

I am getting divorced. I am having regrets now. Not that I feel differently about Adam. But thoughts like these come to mind: Perhaps we will go swimming tomorrow, in my mind I see the three of us, and then I remember there isn't a three of us, there is no family anymore. There is my daughter and me, she has me, she has her father. But not as a family. Not the Three Bears. At first I felt relief and a kind of elation. Now I feel gloomy, sad, and okay too. I guess the parts of my psyche that weren't up to speed are figuring things out.

Memories arise, I think of a day earlier this year; Adam and I went to the beach at Muizenberg without Baby Bear, she was at school or playing with a friend. We couldn't swim together because one of us had to guard the car keys. I watched him walk to the sea, this tall man, in his baggy orange swimming trunks. Who are you? I wondered. How can I spend the rest of my life with you? How will we be, when Kate has grown up and left us alone with each other? At the same time, I felt a strange affection for him, watching him in the waves.

As I am the one asking for the divorce, some of the practical steps are up to me. Adam has moved into the garden cottage on our property and he uses the kitchen in the house, it's a short-term solution. Baby Bear and I have stayed in the house. For now this feels like enough. Although it makes me pleased to see him sometimes, other times I'm annoyed. Just like before, only now there is also the sadness. Before it was either pleased or annoyed. Sometimes at night he dresses up, puts on one of his better shirts and looks as if he is going on a date. He's lost no time. The last thing I would want to do right now is go on a date.

There is a heaviness I am carrying around, in the middle of my body. What is the heaviness? Sometimes it lifts briefly, and then it returns. Soon it will be the holidays and Baby Bear and I will go away for three weeks with friends for the holidays, to our beloved Nieu Bethesda. I am looking forward to this.

In the river
5 December

Deciding to get divorced isn't something you decide to do one day. It happens over a long time, longer than a stormy front, you can feel the barometer falling; a change in air pressure, the sky darkens. It took me years to make the decision.

It has been a big decision. It's like deciding to cross a very wide river; you have to get into it in order to get across. The river is wide and deep and full of currents; the weeds and algae underneath are frightening, slimy and they move. You can't see into the water, it is murky, muddy. There is broken glass.

I am in the river, completely wet, mostly my attention is fixed on getting to the other side, but I have to swim, try not to drown, and not listen to the sirens on the bank behind me beckoning me back.

2012

The benefits of setting fire to your apartment
21 February

Setting fire (inadvertently) to her apartment in the high care unit of the LRR has turned out to be a good thing for Sally. She isn't allowed to smoke in her refurbished apartment anymore, which means she smokes less. She's still going downstairs to get her cigarettes. Of course it is more hassle and she is not in her comfort zone, but she is healthier and happier and more lucid. I keep thinking how things that seem like disasters can turn out to be OK.

It's getting better all the time
30 August

It's six months since I last wrote. My mother is much happier and better now, thanks to the fire. She has to go downstairs to smoke, to get cigarettes. So she has come out of her shell and socialises much more. She watches TV with other people, and she is getting a little exercise from walking along her corridor more times a day. She has cut down on her smoking because of this too.

The process of getting divorced has become easier. I'm happier without the presence of my ex-husband (let me call him that even though we aren't officially divorced yet). I don't have to deal with his moodiness, demands, sulking, and weirdness. Kate and I have a fluid life together, we laugh, talk, read quietly, take our new dog Lucky for a walk each day, eat when supper is ready. There is no panic that supper isn't ready by a particular time, failing which things go pear-shaped. My anxiety levels have dropped to almost nothing most of the time. There are obviously still painful things to deal with, but my daily life has become a lot more pleasant.

One of the unexpected benefits of ending my marriage is that my relationship with my mother has become easier to manage. I have more energy in general. I had her over for the day on Saturday when her carpets had to be cleaned. I didn't dread it as I used to. It was a cold wet Cape Town winter day. I made lunch. We played cards; my mom and my daughter watched a movie, while I had a nap. She was a little mean to Kate a couple of times, in her off-handed way, but I can say Kate was unaffected by her, she isn't open to her granny and she doesn't need her approval. She was kind and patient, even though her gran isn't easy to be with.

False Teeth, ID documents and Christmas
11 September

The seasons are changing and the light earlier in the morning lifts my spirits. Winters in Cape Town can seem endless to those not born here.

I had to fax my mom's ID to the LRR yesterday; they need it for an outing she is going on. Always these tiny (sometimes) admin tasks related to her.

I'm arranging to have false teeth made for her. She recently had most of the teeth in her top jaw removed.

And Christmas. I like to go away at Christmas with Kate and friends, but this year Mike is going to the US with his family to visit Gerry in Florida. And Sean is emigrating to Scotland. So what to do with Mom for Christmas? Gerry has some ideas and we will look into it.

Christmas is a time of guilt. I'm sure I'm not unique in feeling this. That my mom should spend it without family and be at the LRR seems a bit desperate, but not enough for me to give up my annual holiday. It is the one time of the year that is possible to go away for an extended period. Everything closes down or slows down and it's okay to be off duty.

Rinteln, Germany

I'm sleeping in a basement room staying at the house of Wolf, my friend and long lost exchange-student brother. He stayed with my family when he was sixteen. By then I was living in a flat in Rondebosch doing my postgrad teaching diploma at UCT. I shared a flat in Rondebosch with a medical student. My room faced the railway line. The sound of trains coming and going was comforting

Rinteln, Wolf's hometown, offers deep rest after the intense activity of the Frankfurt Book Fair. Short of money, I couldn't pay for my second train ticket back to Frankfurt. Will have to check my bank accounts. Yesterday the weather was lovely in the morning; Wolf and Hanna took me for a drive and a walk in a forest. The forest soil is loamy from centuries of being left alone with its rotting leaves, rain, light, and mushrooms.

Being in Germany feels like having a good parent; the white lines next to the railway lines offer a clear boundary. In every small detail of life here there is a sense of care being taken, of custodianship. Solar panels, wind farms, lights that switch on and off by themselves, activated by a motion sensor.

An ordinary Thursday morning
15 November

On an ordinary Thursday morning before doing the school lift.

- Pack the doll we bought for the Tree of Joy, gift-wrap it first. Remember to purchase said doll the previous day, budget R50, actual cost of doll R140 – where is it possible to buy a doll for R50? Feel guilty that one has overspent and perhaps not done the Right Thing?
- Pack the tablecloth, plate, knife, fork, spoon, salt and pepper, vase, flowers for Afrikaans Oral "Ek dek die tafel".
- Check that swimming togs are packed. Hunt for goggles. Check that 'civvies' for wearing after swimming are packed.
- Sign Homework. Make sure all books are in book bag, including the ones that were left in lounge and bedroom. Make sure child has her glasses.
- Make breakfast, check that teeth are brushed, hair

brushed and tied up.

- Tend to slightly infected splinter wound on foot of child.
- Pack school lunch and extra sandwich for Thursday "bring and share" for poor children who don't have enough to eat.

2013

Talking about birds
4 February

Last week's shopping for my mother: apart from the usual cigarettes, Cokes, and toiletries I bought her some T-shirts from Robelle in Pinelands, an electric fan from Pick n Pay and a bedside reading lamp from the little light shop in Rondebosch. I popped in with the fan, and set it up for her. I've learnt to read instructions and figure out things that are practical. I don't have anyone to ask or do such things for me anymore.

When she called to ask for the fan, we chatted about the guinea fowl she could see from her window. She described their erratic movement and she was eager to tell me that there were chicks. It felt like the first real conversation I have had with her for years. I told her about the flamingoes that have come to the river near where I live, and how the other evening a huge flock wheeled above my head, and then a few landed in the river while most of the flock turned back to where they had come from. I described their long legs and their colours. The pink and white and black of them.

One green budgie
14 March

I love the birds in my neighbourhood; we live close to the Black River. The council workers toil away cleaning the polluted river.

Every day I see some of these birds – starlings, flamingoes, dikkops, waders, seagulls, screaming plovers, swallows, hadedas, egrets, sacred ibises, a heron now and again, lots of small brownish seed-eaters in jittery flocks, crows, doves, pigeons, whiteyes, cormorants. It's a bird sanctuary of sorts, bounded by the motorway, the golf course and the suburb.

At night plovers shriek, disturbed by nightwalkers, they are neighbourhood alarms. Every day I go down to the river with Lucky and there is this whole world of birds we encounter there, decorating the sky, making me lift my eyes. Busy with their own lives. A parallel universe. On my walk today I come across a flock of dowdy wild finches with one bright green budgie amidst them.

The Cape of Storms
15 September

It's been two years since I separated from my almost soon-to-be-ex-husband. We will sign the consent paper next week. Thirteen years after we got married.

The calm, the sanity, the inner peace I feel most of the time nowadays has given me a bigger space to be open to my mother. I see her, I do what I have to for her, and I don't take it personally. I find I love her, I remember that I love her.

Today the weather in Cape Town is wild and stormy, the Cape of Storms. I picture my mother in her place, her small apartment with its classic view of Table Mountain. There won't be much to see today, the weather is close, grey, rainy.

She watches television downstairs now, with other residents (she calls them inmates – her sense of humour dark as always). She has to smoke outside, even in the wild wet weather. There is a shelter and a chair, but no one else smokes with her. She had some smoking friends, but they have gone home. People come to the High Care facility for relatively short periods of 24 hour nursing or when they are recuperating from something. My mother smokes much less now. From three packs of 30s a day, she is down to less than two.

I still don't always pick up when Sally calls, I call her back later. I need to brace myself. But mostly she just calls to say hi, and to ask how Kate is, and what grade she is in, that kind of thing. Sometimes she wants something, and lately she asks for chocolate. Her tastes have changed. She no longer eats fish, now she likes chocolate.

2014

Crocs, Birkenstocks and getting cross
7 September

It's five years since I began this diary. Where is my mother up to? Well she is now 73; she is still living at the Luxury Retirement Resort. I haven't seen her since July. I visited her on her birthday, took her treats and flowers. She is much better, in many ways, but she is still the same, a trickster. She has been caught smoking in her apartment, which sounds like she's in boarding school. Since the fire she may not smoke in her room, for safety reasons. The LRR emailed to ask me to speak to her. I haven't, but I think they are being stricter and more aware of her tricky tendencies.

I had to get her new shoes. Her old pair was falling apart. I wanted to get shoes that at least had a back strap of some sort, as she kept falling or losing her balance in her old beach slops. The Velcro had worn out and wasn't sticking together very well. I tried Crocs, Birkenstocks, Levi tennis shoes – which I cut away at the back. So I had to get shoes and take them to her. I tried Green Cross shoes, leather sandals with Velcro and adjustable straps at the back and across the foot. All this meant me going to a shop, buying the shoes, taking them to my mom and getting her to try them on. I think I must have brought her ten pairs of shoes to try on, but none of them worked for her. She didn't like the brown leather sandals, "they don't go with anything," she said. "They don't match me." She likes shades of blue and that it seems is all.

In the end she got the same kind of shoes again.

I may visit her later today, with three cartons of cigarettes and lighters. Just pop in breezily with the cigarettes, a bunch of flowers and a hug. Still a bit stuck in the old pattern of being aware of her needs, but reluctant to do anything about them. This Sunday is the same, a lovely spring day, crisp air, sunny. And a weighed down feeling inside. The complex. My complex. My mother complex.

2015

My real neighbours
29 April

My real neighbours are birds. People's sounds are harsher, more discordant, argumentative, a hoot, a car revving, a door slams, siren wails. I hear the birds all day long, and at night too. The water birds crying at the river, their calls rising like mist. Tiny whiteyes, crows, doves watching from the wires, checking that I turn where I always do.

Just before I feed the dog, the pigeons arrive; they sit on the roof, waiting patiently.

Sometimes flamingoes fly overhead. A soft squadron, black crosses in the sky. They drift down, feet first into the river. No splash.

The birds make daily music, small guardian angels. They take pleasure in the sprinkler splashing leaves, dripping onto their feathers; they shake and bustle.

In winter they feast on the orange aloe petals, in summer tuck into the honeysuckle and later the ripening pink peppercorns. The plovers dive-bomb us when we walk at the river, threatening us to keep away.

Suburban doves, sparrows, sunbirds, starlings – singly or in flocks. Hadedas, Egyptian geese in couples. My neighbours.

Thick glass
4 May

Drowning quietly, thick glass between the world and me. Can't breathe. Too heavy, too much. I'm full of rage, desperation.

2016

Bridge of sighs
6 January

My mother is a bridge of sighs, a slightly creaking structure that has to be watched carefully, lest it collapses, but her secret is that she is strong, virtually indestructible. It seems no amount of self-abuse can harm her.

My father was more mysterious, less scrutinised, a less visible presence, one we took for granted, like a tree, but he is gone now, felled. Dead. What did he sound like? Sometimes he'd tell jokes and he'd laugh so much that tears would roll down his cheeks.

Salivary gland infection
4 June

My mom is in hospital with an infection in her salivary gland, after a visit to the dentist. Till last night, I didn't even know this was a thing. I also didn't know that you could get stones in your salivary gland, not just in gall bladders and kidneys. She's getting better; the antibiotics in an IV drip are doing their work.

All her teeth
21 July

On Monday I am taking my mother to an oral maxilla

surgeon to have all her teeth out. It sounds like something that would come up in a dream, "My mother has lost all her teeth". If it was a dream it could mean she has lost her bite, she can't eat me up anymore, I'm no longer afraid of her.

In reality she is an old woman, and the only food she will be able to eat will be mushy or liquid. She won't like it. She will grumble once it has happened, she hasn't thought through what it will mean. She doesn't have a choice though, her remaining teeth are basically rotten, 'vrot' (her word). The infection in her salivary gland was probably because of these teeth; it happened after her last visit to the dentist.

Kate is in high school now; it's a big change. I feel as though I've lost my bearings again.

I've come a long way with my mother, inside of myself. It was her birthday this past weekend, and we went with Mike and his family to have lunch with her at the Club at the LRR. She loved it, in spite of herself. And because of modern technology she was able to speak to Sean in Scotland and to Gerry in Florida. She was thrilled. Even now I can picture her talking to them on my phone, her Coke in front of her, her wheelie walker in the background.

Inner and outer, the end and the beginning
25 November

A few weeks ago, Sally was hospitalised. She was severely dehydrated, which compromised her kidney function. She had a bladder infection and was delirious. She got better slowly after spending nearly two weeks in hospital.

She is still in frail care. She was in rehab, first. These categories have more to do with the medical aid, what they will pay, how much and for how long, than about an actual space she is in. It is the same LRR.

At first she was barely mobile, and even now she has trouble getting up. She has to use her walker, but it is not stable enough for her, the wheels move.

The move from assisted living to frail care is a big one; there is no semblance of independence in frail care. I'm still hoping she will be able to go back to assisted living, meaning her small apartment on the third floor with the view of Table Mountain.

"Is my flat still there? And my things?"

"Yes, yes, they are – they are waiting for you to come back."

"Why am I here?" she asks. "How come I am living in this place?"

"Is it something to do with TPS?" (The last place she worked: 25 years ago.)

"No, you are retired. I say. You don't have to work."

"Oh, I must be rich then!"

"Yes you are, I guess."

Much richer than most people in South Africa. I don't say that bit out loud. It's a mantra I say to myself, when I feel that my life is hard, and that things aren't going well for me. So I don't feel too sorry for myself.

When she is in hospital she speaks Sesotho to the nurses and to me. When the Rwandan nurse doesn't respond, my mother thinks the nurse is being cold. I tell her, when the nurse leaves, that she doesn't know Sesotho, she is Rwandan. She looks at me with her one eyebrow raised. Disbelieving.

One day she tells me that she never wants to see me again when she gets out of hospital. She blames me for everything about her life that she doesn't like. The things that overwhelm her make her feel out of control. "You should have left me to die. I wish I had died," she says.

I take this to analysis and think about it at odd moments after that. Our excellent care for old people means they live longer than they used to, she would have died if she hadn't gone to hospital and been put on a drip with antibiotics and rehydrating fluids. I am deeply relieved, in spite of everything, that she has survived a little longer.

The day after she is admitted she has to have an ultrasound of her kidney. She only has one. The other was removed when she was in what I think of as her Munchausen's phase. I go with her down the endless undifferentiated corridors; an orderly wheels her on her bed to the ultrasound section.

"What is your surname?" She asks him. His first name is on a name badge on his chest.

"Cloete," he says. "What is yours?"

"I don't have one." A little smile makes her look as though she got away with something.

We are in the dark, my mother wearing the hospital garment, and an adult nappy. The ultrasound technician puts the gel onto her abdomen. She moves the wand over her tummy; I remember ultrasounds I have had, after mammograms, and when I was pregnant. The technician talks about "the bed of the missing kidney". There is just

111

space, absence. And near the empty space, the remaining kidney has grown bigger to compensate for the missing one. I see the screen, and feel as though I am falling into space, inner space, which reminds me of nothing so much as images of outer space, with whorls and darknesses and flickers of stars, and deep mysterious workings of which I know very little. In spite of the expensive high tech medical equipment, I wonder if the doctors and scientists know as much as we think they do of inner space, the inner workings of the human body.

As I look into the ultrasound image I think, once I lived there inside you, Mom. I grew from a microscopic speck, and now the ground of my being, you my mother, the ground of my being, you will die, both of us will die. One day. I feel tears on my face, my heart aches, and I miss her already. I miss myself and I miss Kate.

Like a river
14 December

A nurse came today to do a medical for my new life insurance company. So much story was evoked by her questions. But the story isn't the stuff the insurance company wants to know. Story and subtext. The time I had a lumpectomy at 19. They wanted a three page report completed by my doctor. He died a long time ago, in the late 80s. He was brutally murdered in a home invasion. What was the exact diagnosis, the size of tumour?

They want to know why I still see a psychoanalyst after

all these years (I started in 1988). What was the trigger? How many episodes of depression have you had since then? Well it's not like that. For me going to therapy is a good habit, like exercise and brushing my teeth, it helps me to live well and be happy and be a good enough parent. And to not get sick with all kinds of somatised illnesses. The nurse was friendly and made the best of my responses. But for me it was like a river, all the things beneath the surface.

2017

Emergency Room
25 March

My mother got better after her illness, although she was frailer. It took time for her to get back to herself, but she was able to move back to her apartment and was walking about using her wheelie walker. Her ankles were painfully swollen. They cut her hair as it had become matted when she was in hospital, so she looked more like the person I was familiar with; long thin hair in a ponytail was strange for a woman like my mother. She'd recently got new dentures; she'd lost her upper dentures in the previous hospitalisation episode.

The evening before last I went to the Milnerton Mediclinic with Kate, just a visit to see my mom in hospital again. But when we arrived on the ward there was a scene from ER going on. The curtains were drawn – there was a swarm of people busy with her and there were all kinds of machines and beeping noises and people rushing out and rushing back.

The doctor emerged from the curtains, "She has had heart failure," he said. "We resuscitated her after three attempts." He asked me to consider if they should resuscitate her if "she went again". I felt panicky; it was hard to breathe. What was the right answer? I didn't know. He told me he was taking her into the ICU and he told me what he would do for her. I couldn't really make head or tail of what he said. I heard words as though I was hearing a foreign language that I only vaguely understood. Ruptured ulcer. Heart failure. Kidney failure. Vomiting. Ventilator. Resuscitate.

He asked me if I had someone who could come and be with me. A sibling. A friend. I understood only then that he meant this was very serious. That I would need support. I called my friend, also Colleen, who has effectively been Kate's granny. She left her pottery class and came with her friend Marijke, who was also at pottery. Marijke took Kate to get something to eat. She hadn't had supper. My sister in law, Gaye Lisa, and my niece Megan arrived too.

Eventually, after my mother had been in the ICU for nearly two hours, the doctor came out and told us what had happened, what he now suspected and what he was planning to do. He was calm and kind and clear. It seems she had a perforated small intestine and this had infected her whole body. Her kidney had failed, her blood pressure was very low, and her body was 10 times more acidic than it should have been. She had effectively been vomiting up the contents of her small intestine. He said there was a single digit percentage that she might recover from this, and he could not say what her neurological function would be.

He said many other things that I don't remember. I remember kindness. Calm. The kind of love that strangers can have for other strangers, because they are human too.

Gone

25 March

After the doctor told us what to expect, Kate went to my friend Colleen's home and I stayed with Gaye and Megan. We went in to see her in the ICU. She was lying flat on her back. She was not conscious. She looked tiny and shrunken under the bedclothes and was attached to many machines and tubes and lines. She was being put onto dialysis as we came in to see her. They had taped her eyes shut. They had not been able to clean her hair, sticky from vomiting.

My mother lying in the hospital bed. I knew (I think I knew) it was her deathbed. I touched her head. I told her I loved her. I stroked her forehead; I patted her arm through the bedclothes. They told me she was very cold. Gaye was able to understand the numbers on the machine – I had no idea what I was seeing, I could see colours and numbers, but once again, it was utterly incomprehensible to me.

There was some beeping and intensity, and then the doctor told us she was gone. He said sorry. The nurses said sorry. We went outside to the waiting area. I was numb.

Gaye phoned Gerry. While she was on the phone the doctor came out and told us that my mother had come back, she was breathing again, her heart was beating again.

★★★

We went back in, stood next to her bed. After a while we returned to the waiting room. I decided to go home to get my phone charger as my phone's battery had almost run out. I would stay at the hospital all night; I knew she was going to die that night. When I got back, Gaye and Megan left. They live in Kommetjie, a long way to the Milnerton Mediclinic.

It was now about 12.30. I lay down in the patients' lounge on a couch. The night manager sister kindly brought me a duvet and pillow. I slept in short patches for half an hour or forty minutes at a time. I kept expecting the nurses to come and tell me that my mother had died.

At about 4 in the morning, one of the sisters came and told me she wasn't doing too well. I went through. Her blood pressure was very low. I said, "It's Ok Mom, you can go. You will be able to be with Dad now." I didn't believe rationally that was what would happen. But I said it and meant it. Death is a mystery.

After I had been there for about fifteen minutes, the nurses told me again they were sorry. She has gone. She has gone. I touched her on the forehead, kissed her there.

I looked around. This was not a good place to die. I don't know how aware she was of her surroundings, of where she was. The flashing lights, the noise, the beeps, the tubes, and lines, the machines. The high-techness of it all. She hadn't wanted to come to the hospital, I heard later. She had to be persuaded, coerced. I think she knew she was going to die and she didn't want to have yet another ambulance ride, the ICU.

★★★

The nurses told me they would clean her up and then I could come and be with her. "Can you let the family know? Or do you want us to?" I said I would. I called Gaye. She called Gerry and Mike. I phoned Sean in Scotland.

★★★

Her death struck me the most deeply several hours later, when I finally went back to see her. The nurses had been waiting to hear from the doctor. There are protocols, they couldn't do anything to her until he gave the go-ahead. The tubes were gone; the tape over her eyes was gone. She looked more herself now than she had before, but she was cold. I touched her again. Mom. Mom.

The sisters brought me several cups of tea; I had to sign for her rings and a big plastic bag filled with her meds. Boxes and boxes of pills for all of her conditions and illnesses. I cried and couldn't stop for a long time.

It was morning traffic, a beautiful autumn morning. I drove down Koeberg Road, towards Table Mountain. My mother is gone. The mountain she could see from her apartment and the view she did love in spite of herself came closer and closer as I drove home.

★★★

I feel strange, not quite myself, I find it hard to really concentrate on what people are saying, my ability to concentrate comes and goes. I feel heaviness in the centre of my body. I'm glad it was quick, the end, and that my mother did not have to live for a long time in frail care, or some kind of nursing situation, in the liminal space between life and death. It was quick and she is gone, and she did not suffer for long in the end.

Oh Mom.

Indian summer

18 April

It's almost a month later. Even in death my mother defies me. I have had many expressions of condolences and I'm thankful for them, it means that there are people who have noticed enough to say something. And many of the expressions are kind and caring. However, I can't take them into my heart in a simple open way. My relationship with my mother was so fraught and complicated that even now I don't feel plain grief.

Part of what I'm grappling with: Is she really gone? How can this be? I know I was with her when she died. I saw the last breath leave her body. I saw her body in the funeral parlour, her mouth looked like a beak; she didn't have her dentures in. Her beautiful cheekbones and high forehead were visible, but she wasn't lovely in death, she had dark rings around her eyes, as though she had been in a fight.

My oldest connection to life, to my life is gone. Even though I feel something of a relief that the burden of caring for her has been lifted from me, even though I feel lighter, I'm still grappling with what her death means.

We have celebrated her life twice now – once with her friends and family from the Fish Hoek area at the Glencairn golf course, and once at the Luxury Retirement Resort – where we were able to thank the staff and acknowledge her life with the other "inmates" as she called them.

We buried her ashes at Silvermine on the ridge that overlooks Cape Town and False Bay. My siblings were here and we did it together. We buried her near where we buried the ashes of David, her husband, our father. There was something satisfying about doing all the right things, getting the needful things done. I like the thought that she and David have a lovely view from where their ashes are buried. They can look down onto False Bay, the sea.

Life goes on. We're having a glorious Indian Summer here in Cape Town, the rains still have not come, the drought continues. If you didn't know about the drought, you would be able to simply enjoy the exquisite days.

It takes time
4 May

Was shopping for a few things for Kate yesterday late afternoon at Woollies in Cavendish. I nearly turned to her to say, "Granny Sally would like that." A blue cotton shirt. It takes time for all the parts of my psyche to remember that she has died.

I thought I'd lost her rings, but this morning while hunting for nail clippers (which I didn't find) her rings were in my underwear drawer. They weren't lost after all.

2018

The lost father
25 April

Yesterday in the last few minutes of therapy, I realised how Philip's philandering ways would have affected me as a small child. He wouldn't have been home as much as a faithful father would have. He wouldn't have had the focus. He would have driven Sally crazier than she actually was. Somehow I'd kept all the bits separate. Sally's breakdown, my loss of Philip – they weren't discrete isolated pieces of personal history.

I'd survived on one photograph and a lot of fantasy. In the picture, Sally and Philip are each holding a child, Sean and me. The only person smiling is Philip. Sally and Philip have paper hats, from Christmas crackers, on their heads. Who took the photo? As a child I would often take the picture out, to look at Philip (I had Sean and Sally in real life). I would try and see into the picture. It was deeply unsatisfying, but it had just enough mystery and promise to keep me returning to it. It was all that was left of Philip, the lost father.

What kind of person are you?
27 October

I think of my mother sometimes when I am going through an ordinary day, going to the gate to check the post, driving up Klipfontein Road to fetch Kate at school, waiting at a robot, pushing a trolley in the shops. I imagine visiting her, popping out to Century City, to go and have a cup of tea with her. Not that there was anything in it for me. After I'd visited I was likely to feel tired and weak and need to lie down.

I picture her sitting in her small apartment watching television, smoking and drinking Coke; the carpet around her comfortable recliner chair dirty and stained from her spills and ash. At her windows hang the lovely embroidered heavy creamy curtains with the pink and orange embroidered flowers I had made especially for her flat, and through the windows there is a magnificent view of Table Mountain. Mothers can't live by views alone, I hear a voice say in my head. Another voice whispers back fiercely, It's you or her.

My mother was not very old; just over 20 years older than me. She had early onset senile dementia, she was bipolar, she needed care, she couldn't take care of herself. Sometimes I glimpsed a sweet bright person through the cloudy, murky, washed-up person who read *You* magazine, who always complained. Cokes and cigarettes were the refrain of my mother's life, complaint and repetition the melody.

In the years before we realised she needed care, she did some very weird things, she would go shopping in her pajamas, she didn't eat properly. She lived in a road in Fish Hoek where everyone's house was painted either white or cream, or at its most colourful, pale lemon. My mother painted her house cerise, she painted a frenzy of colourful flowers on her garage, she painted the inside vibacrete walls bright orange, she planted a wild garden filled with gnomes, stone frogs, metal birds, bird baths, tortoises – an enchanted secret crazy garden bursting with colour and life. And some days she would harvest sleeping pills and Syndols from pharmacies where she was still served even if it meant driving to Tokai and Wynberg first. Then she would take a small overdose, not enough to kill her, but enough to knock her out for a few days.

Her neighbours wrote her hate mail, they accused her of bringing down the tone of the neighbourhood. She loved the attention. She would phone me and read me the letters, sounding both aggrieved and victorious.

It was a big shift for me to realise I had to be responsible for my mother, especially when she had been a black hole of ambivalence for most of my life.

Once we were coming back from a holiday driving on that last stretch back into Cape Town, where you can see Table Mountain ahead, and Century City comes up on the right. Kate was asleep in the back. I said to Adam, "You're lucky your mother is dead." He turned, looked at me shocked, and said, "What kind of a person are you?" There are many things that he didn't forgive me for, and my sometimes wishing that my mother was dead was one of them.

When you have a mother like Sally, how do you recover? How do you make something of your life that isn't all about suffering, reluctance, resistance, bushels and hiding under them. Sally is what there was. She was my mother, the roots that fed me as I grew.

2019

Especially not the lawn
25 March

Sally died exactly two years ago. And today someone named Karen came and fetched the canopy for Adam's Mahindra bakkie. It's been sitting there for the eight years that our marriage has been over. She also took the lawnmower. The drought and water restrictions mean I will never have need for a lawnmower in my Cape Flats garden. Here the grass dies in the summer and the sand shifts and rises, and only some things grow, but not the lawn, especially not the lawn if you can't put sprinklers on twice a day. The drying wind sucks up the moisture from the soil, the overcast days trigger gloominess. Sunny days are too hot and bright. The restlessness of the wind.

Acknowledgements

Thank you to Robert Berold of Deep South for editing this memoir in his sensitive and careful way, and for publishing it.

A special thanks to Colleen Crawford Cousins, my dear friend, for all the writing and talking and processing of what I have written here, and much more besides.

To Kate, for teaching me to be her mother, for opening my heart wide, and I hope into being more or less 'good enough'.

Thank you to the staff of the Luxury Retirement Resort for looking after my mother and containing her in the last ten years of her life. Their patience, kindness, and appreciation of her made a huge difference to her, and to me.

Finally, I thank Renee Ramsden, who sat with me and helped me to make sense of all of this. Who listened to my dreams, helped me to understand them, made it possible for me to take myself on and become more objective about my mother and about myself. Who helped me to love my mother more calmly in the last ten years of her life.

Printed in the United States
By Bookmasters